COLLINS

SCOTLAND WORLD CUP GUIDE '98

Text by Chris Dighton and Hayters

Collins
Willow

Contents

Team Preview

France 1998

Introduction

THE DRAW MAY BE TOUGH – but who can argue with the hand of fate that sets up such a dream tie? Scotland v Brazil, the champions – the game to kick off the 1998 World Cup in the stadium of stadiums, the Stade de France at St Denis, Paris on Wednesday 10 June 1998. And fear not, brave hearts. Given that there are no easy ways to win a World Cup, why not jump in at the deep end? It is simple: to be the best you've got to beat the best. Positive thinking is the order of the day and there is much to savour. Consider the spin-offs from this game: a dream chance to impress a global TV audience that will be the biggest ever; a chance to make an early impression and send shock waves through the rest of the tournament; a chance to be a match away from qualifying for the knockout rounds before the other 30 teams have kicked a ball in anger. Think right and it all becomes rather a tasty prospect.

'It's a great honour to play the opening game,' said Craig Brown, the Scotland coach. 'We have played against Brazil three times during previous World Cups and have lost and logically Brazil should be first in Group A.'

But was there ever a better time and place to upset logic? Remember Cameroon in 1990, upsetting champions Argentina 1-0 in the opening game. And then remember what Cameroon went on to achieve – a place in the quarter-finals.

This is Scotland's eighth trip to the World Cup finals since 1954 and, as always, the first hurdle is to reach the second stage. It is painful to record, as it has been far too often in the past, that not once has this hurdle been cleared. Maybe this time....

Despite Scotland's history there is hope, there are memories of great victories and there is a team spirit in the camp that will not yield. This Scotland squad of '98 is one that knows hard work will be rewarded; they will not be seduced by a battle cry of false optimism, nor will they give up the fight until the bitter end.

Fighting it out with them in Group A are Morocco and Norway, and as Brown noted, those sides register higher in the FIFA rankings than Scotland.

'We have no inferiority complex and our realistic aim is to finish second,' said Brown.

A qualifying route that brought good wins over Austria (who have also reached France '98) and Sweden was made better by the performance of a defence that conceded just three goals in ten games. And as the pattern of World Cup football proves, the days of high-scoring matches are long gone, the golden rule is to keep it tight at the back and then look for goals from that base.

It will be hard but nobody expects anything different – and Scotland are certainly going to make it difficult for Brazil and everybody else they meet.

So settle back and prepare for the greatest show on earth, a feast of football. Scotland are dining at the high table and the time is right for them to make it through to the second course – enjoy the action.

Craig Brown

The job advert was simple: Wanted — Manager to take charge of Scotland.

On the surface it seems an attractive proposition, offering travel, kudos and the potential for glory. Look ahead though, and suddenly the job loses its rosy hue. For hand in hand with the advantages come demanding fans, a database of players that is, perhaps, a bit thin and a history that is tarnished by a certain unenviable tradition – through the seven World Cup finals for which Scotland have qualified, they have never made it further than the first round.

None of this, however, deters Craig Brown, the apprentice turned manager, the so-so player whose career ended after five knee operations in the early 1960s. By that time he had been in Dundee's League winning side of 1962 and finished his playing days at Falkirk. During his time as a player, Craig was not the only member of the Brown family involved in the game – his brother Jock, now general manager at Celtic FC, was a commentator for Scottish football, often interviewing Craig after a game.

The transition from player to coach was not immediate, and after retiring from the game Brown returned to the profession he had put on hold when football beckoned – teaching. He eventually became headmaster of a primary school, but his association with the game was not over, and he was lured back with offers of managerial positions.

He started out as assistant manager at Motherwell, then moved on to become manager of part-timers Clyde, but the national sides needed his services and

Brown soon took charge of the Scotland junior sides, at Under-16, Under-18 and Under-21 levels. Gradually he progressed through the ranks, and served as assistant to Alex Ferguson during his caretaker spell as Scotland manager in 1985–86, and then later became the right-hand man to Andy Roxburgh, Scotland manager from 1986 to 1993.

Brown will admit that when the post became vacant he wasn't exactly the name to the fore when replacements were being hunted. Those that topped a poll in a Scottish daily newspaper were Alex Ferguson, George Graham, Graeme Souness, Bruce Rioch, Rab C. Nesbitt, Kenneth McKeller and Gavin Hastings. Yet Brown was the man to emerge with the job in September 1993. Qualification for Euro '96 and the World Cup in France are proof that he is doing something right.

At heart he is a fan – albeit a fan with a reputation as a great coach – and what happens to Scotland matters a lot. This is a man who starts his programme notes with the line: 'Dear fellow supporter....' He has visited prisons and held Q & A sessions on the team with inmates; he has flown out to oil rigs to do the same thing; and on the odd occasion he has invited abusive letter-writers to pop in and see him in his Glasgow office to have a cup of tea and a chat. If there is any way Brown can raise the team's profile and further their cause, he will go out of his way to do it.

'Supporting Scotland is like being married to a woman who's got a permanent headache,' he says. 'You're always out looking for something and you always get nothing.'

Talk of getting nothing shifts the focus onto the Scotland defence – here opponents of real quality find that the Scots have given little away of late. They came through a ten-match qualifying programme conceding just three goals.

The results of Brown's dedication and inspiration are there for all to see: he has fostered a tremendous team spirit, and in the process has built a Scotland side stronger than the sum of its parts. Now in his late fifties, he is a no-nonsense man with an avuncular image, he handles his players with a firm but fair hand, and never criticizes them in public or in front of their colleagues. He is loyal to his players and they pay him back in kind. For all that, he is no fool and will not let expectations for France build up to absurd proportions. This has happened in previous Scotland World Cup campaigns and the thud of disappointment has been made all the harder because of it.

The hope is there, however, and it cannot be denied that progressing through the first stage would be a major triumph for the country and for Brown, turning the man who prompted the question, 'Who?' when he was first appointed, into a revered household name.

Tommy Boyd

Club: Celtic
Previous clubs: Motherwell, Chelsea
Height: 5'11"
Born: 24 November 1965
International debut: v Romania 2-1
  (Glasgow) 16 October 1990

'I love playing in top games and I'd do anything to be involved in France '98.'

Tommy Boyd will probably be far more comfortable flying to France than going south to England, because the memories of his time in London are likely to be more frightening than the prospect of boarding an aeroplane.

Boyd had just a handful of caps for Scotland when he made what seemed to be a dream move to Chelsea for £800,000. That was in May 1991, and in February 1992 Boyd was on his way back north to Celtic. The dream move had turned into a nightmare. Boyd did not like Chelsea and Chelsea could not have felt much better about him. The defender was swapped for Tony Cascarino, a deal which does little to describe the worth of Boyd to Celtic or Scotland.

Last year Boyd's contribution and service to the Bhoys were rewarded with the captaincy. He was a popular and inevitable choice. If ever there was a man who could replace Paul McStay, then Boyd was that man. In six years with Celtic he has never appeared to give less than his best; through four managers, countless comings and goings in player personnel. In what has seemed at times a hopeless quest for glory, Boyd has been one of the few rock-solid foundations at Celtic Park.

His reliability has not just been confined to domestic football; he won his 50th cap in the final World Cup qualifier against Latvia last year. He was substituted with ten minutes left on the clock, so that the faithful could express their gratitude for seven years of sterling work. It was a far cry from Boyd's first game for Scotland against Romania, when he received the call-up because of a glut of injuries in the squad. He became one of the élite group of Motherwell players who have represented their country, but from the minute he stepped on the pitch it was clear that he would not be a Motherwell player for much longer.

Boyd kept his place in the Scotland team even when all the injuries had long since healed, and at 32 this is probably his last chance to grab all the headlines that he has been denied in seven years of quietly impressive football.

Craig Burley

Club: Celtic
Previous clubs: Chelsea, Hogabog BK, Helsingborgs BK
Height: 6'1"
Born: 24 September 1971
International debut: v Japan 0-0
(Hiroshima) 21 May 1995

*'The night before a game, I try not to think about it at all.
But on the day, I usually have about five superstitions
I have to go through.'*

Craig Burley has had more than his fair share of
cups and downs. Before joining Celtic the
hard-working midfielder spent as much time on
the sidelines as on the pitch, with a combination of
injuries and bad luck conspiring to make his time at
Chelsea less than fulfilling. Having joined the London
club straight from Youth level in 1989, he finally
established himself in the first team in the 1993-94
season. A series of injuries, however, interrupted his
progress in 1995 and he was left out of the club's
triumphant 1997 FA Cup Final squad.

Despite the regular interruptions to his career,
Burley has always impressed when given the chance.
He has been capped at all levels for Scotland, earning
his first full cap under Craig Brown in 1995, and he
was an important member of Scotland's Euro '96 squad.

The nephew of
Ipswich manager George
Burley, Craig admits
that having a family
connection in the game
has been helpful.

'Although he
wasn't responsible for me
becoming a professional –
that has more to do with
my dad Tom – George
has been full of good
advice, especially when
I first came into the
game. After all, he has
experience of playing at
the top level and has seen
it all. It was good to ask
him about stuff that
goes on both on and
off the pitch.'

Now fully fit, Burley has played the most
consistent football of his career since joining Celtic in
a deal worth some £2.5 million last summer.

'I came here to win things,' he said and soon
proved his point, scoring in Celtic's 3-0 Coca-Cola
Cup Final victory against Dundee United. It made up
for missing out at Wembley, although Burley looks
back at that omission philosophically:

'I think being left out for the Final against
Middlesbrough was perhaps a blessing in disguise. It
forced me to realize the time was right to move on.
I've certainly enjoyed my football since I came to
Celtic. Two draws with Liverpool proved we could
compete with the best and I've grown in confidence
since I've been playing in Scotland. I always felt like
a fringe player down south. No matter how often
I played, I always had the suspicion I was about to
be dropped.'

The new-found confidence was evident in
Burley's performances for Scotland during the World
Cup qualifiers.

Colin Calderwood

Club: Tottenham Hotspur
Previous clubs: Mansfield Town, Swindon Town
Height: 6'0"
Born: 20 January 1965
International debut: v Russia 0-0
(Moscow) 29 March 1995

'He is a class defender playing against class strikers every week.'
Scotland manager Craig Brown on Calderwood.

Colin Calderwood has come a long way since forcing his way into a struggling Mansfield Town side way back in the early 1980s, at the age of 17. Even in the lower divisions he had to learn his trade fast and, almost two decades on, he is finally reaping the benefits of his long apprenticeship.

One of the surviving members of Scotland's Euro '96 squad, Calderwood is one of football's quieter men off the pitch. On it, however, he is a tower of strength and his contribution to the team's impressive World Cup qualification campaign should not be underestimated. Scotland conceded just three goals in ten games *en route* to France.

A life-long Rangers fan, he has had to wait until the twilight of his career to fulfil the potential that

helped Swindon Town clinch the Fourth Division championship in 1986 as well as promotion to the Premiership in 1993. Sadly for Swindon, Calderwood did not hang around to sample the club's first and only season in the top-flight. After helping them beat Leicester in the play-off final, he transferred to Tottenham for £1.25 million. Without him, Swindon struggled and was relegated, conceding a disastrous 100 goals on their way down.

At Spurs Calderwood initially struggled to make an impact, and within a year of his arrival Ossie Ardiles agreed to sell him to Celtic at a knockdown price. It was only the sacking of manager Lou Macari 24 hours after the deal had been struck which scuppered the move. Celtic Park's loss proved to be White Hart Lane's gain.

He has shown a new-found versatility this season, helping Tottenham overcome its crippling injury list by operating in midfield. For a player who once said, 'I don't think I fancy myself in any other position than a defender,' it has not been an easy transition, but he has taken to the role with his trademark determination and professionalism.

Scotland manager Craig Brown knows Calderwood will be nothing if not consistent in France. Strong in the air and superbly fit, the Tottenham stopper may not be the man to completely shut out Ronaldo and the rest of his Brazilian team-mates but you can guarantee he will make them work hard for their chances.

John Collins

Club: Monaco
Previous clubs: Hibernian, Celtic
Height: 5'7"
Born: 31 January 1968
International debut: v Saudi Arabia 2-2
(Riyadh) 17 February 1988

'My performance against Holland in Euro '96 was one of the best games I've had for Scotland.'

It is unlikely anyone in the Scotland squad is more *au fait* with France than John Collins. The former Celtic midfielder has now completed two seasons of football with Monaco.

Collins was one of the first British players to take advantage of the Bosman Ruling. When his contract with Celtic expired, he arranged a move to France said to be worth some £2.5 million over three years.

'I am lucky to be a player at the time of the Bosman business,' he admitted. 'It's the best thing that could have happened for me. Yet I resent people calling me greedy. I made enough money playing for Celtic to be considered comfortable and they did have opportunities to sell me.'

Not that Scotland coach Craig Brown is too concerned about big money deals. All he is interested in is Collins' form. And that has been excellent both for Scotland and Monaco.

'I think John's benefited from the move to France,' admits Brown. 'The fact that a club like Monaco were so keen to sign him, and prepared to offer an extremely attractive contract, has done a lot for his confidence.'

Another admirer of Collins is England boss Glenn Hoddle, who recommended the player to Monaco after failing to sign him for Chelsea. It's hardly surprising that Hoddle would be a fan – some of Collins' work bears an uncanny resemblance to his own playing skills.

A cultured midfielder with good vision, Collins takes a mean free-kick and is also an excellent tackler. Born in the Borders town of Galashiels, he could have pursued a career in rugby like many of the locals, but instead he opted for football – a decision that has been well vindicated. He was with Scotland in the 1990 World Cup finals, and the 1992 European Championships in Sweden, but was used mostly wide on the left by then-manager Andy Roxburgh. He has flourished, however, since Brown moved him to a more central role. He was one of Scotland's best players in the run-up to Euro '96, performed well in the tournament, and was a mainstay in qualification for France '98. And Brown has admitted that Collins' local knowledge could prove a valuable asset this summer.

Christian Dailly

Club: Derby County
Previous clubs: Dundee United
Height: 6'0"
Born: 23 October 1973
International debut: v Wales 0-1
(Kilmarnock) 27 May 1997

'Derby County have definitely toughened me up and I am a much stronger player now.'

Christian Dailly was what you might call an early developer. While his teenage contemporaries were still pursuing more typically adolescent goals, he was forcing his way into senior football and breaking Scottish records like there was no tomorrow.

Incredibly, he made his Dundee United debut at the age of 16 and in the same year he broke into the Scotland Under-21 side – the youngest player ever to make the grade. His tally of 34 caps at that level is still a national record. Now 24, Dailly is already something of a seasoned veteran.

The Dundee-born midfielder-cum-defender spent six seasons at Tannadice, playing in over 100 League games for the Tangerines before heading south of the border, although it was nearly in the blue of Manchester City rather than the white of Derby County that he resurfaced. Keen to kick-start his career in the summer of 1996, Dailly had hoped for a free transfer to Maine Road under the Bosman ruling, but Dundee United stalled the move and it seemed he was staying in Scotland. Derby manager Jim Smith had other ideas, however, and decided he was worth £1 million.

He began life at Derby as the midfield anchorman, but when Croatian international Igor Stimac was injured, Dailly switched to the heart of the defence. It was this versatility that alerted Craig Brown, and he gave him his Scotland debut in a friendly against Wales in May 1997, after injuries deprived him of the services of the two Colins – Hendry and Calderwood.

Dailly obviously relished the promotion to the full side, and scored his first goal for Scotland in his second full international a week later against Malta. His elevation to the international stage helped Dailly at club level and he completed his first season with the Rams strongly, missing just two of their Premiership outings.

A broken jaw and Derby's impressive Premiership form have meant first-team opportunities have been limited for the young Scot in 1997–98 but, despite nearly a decade in senior football to his name, he still has time on his side and the incentive of a trip to the greatest football show on earth to motivate him.

Billy Dodds

Club: Aberdeen
Previous clubs: Chelsea, Partick Thistle (loan), Dundee, St Johnstone
Height: 5'8"
Born: 5 February 1969
International debut: v Latvia 2-0 (Riga) 5 October 1996

'There's a list of six strikers competing for Scotland places and I'm sixth.'

If Billy Dodds achieves little else in a Scotland shirt he is assured a place in their history by the infamous events of 8 October 1996. For it was on that day that Dodds and Scotland were involved in the match that never was. Three days earlier the 28-year-old Aberdeen striker had proudly won his first full Scotland cap as a substitute for John Spencer in the hard-earned 2-0 victory over Latvia. In Tallinn he was

chosen to play against Estonia ... but Dodds' long-awaited first start in Scotland's dark blue jersey turned into farce. He takes up the story: 'I was really proud to have been selected from the start but I smelled a rat after I'd pulled on my Scotland jersey and ran out for the warm-up.

'There wasn't a single fan in the ground so we guessed something was up. Until then we had no clue anything was wrong. It was totally bizarre, the strangest feeling of my life. I kicked-off, John Collins took a couple of touches and it was all over. I didn't know whether to laugh or cry. It occurred to me it might be my only chance to start an international – and it didn't count.'

That was because opponents Estonia failed to turn up after a row with FIFA over kick-off times. Dodds had to sit out the rearranged Estonia match in Monaco because of injury, but got back in against Wales later that season. Yet he is aware he cannot take anything for granted. 'I still have to prove myself but I am ready for the fight,' he said.

Dodds scored 15 goals for Aberdeen last season but was hit by tragedy this term when sister Barbara was killed in a car crash. He has given his Scottish employers sterling service after failing to make the grade in England. In three seasons with Chelsea he played only three League games, and it needed a spell on loan at Partick Thistle to kick-start his career. Dodds claimed nine goals in 30 League games, alerting Dundee to his potential, and in 1989 he moved to Dens Park. In the best of five seasons there he netted 19 League goals, a figure he has yet to match in three seasons at Pittodrie.

Simon Donnelly

Club: Celtic
Previous clubs: Queens Park
Height: 5'9"
Born: 1 December 1974
International debut: v Wales 0-1
(Kilmarnock) 27 May 1997

'If it hadn't been for football I would probably still be slaving away on a business course at Motherwell College.'

It cannot be easy to justify the label when someone compares you to a legend before you have reached your 23rd birthday. But that is the awesome task confronting Celtic striker Simon Donnelly, who grapples with the burden of being compared to the great Kenny Dalglish. The immortal Kenny, of course, collected enough honours to fill half a dozen sideboards during his distinguished playing career and goes on adding to them as a manager. But it is hardly a fair comparison. Dalglish scored 30 goals during a 15-year Scotland career which yielded a record 102 caps.

Donnelly's international career began quietly with a total of 21 minutes' experience as substitute against Wales, Latvia and France, and he would be the first to acknowledge that he has a long way to go to live up to the Dalglish label. His first four seasons in the Celtic first team hardly provided figures to justify this tag; in 93 League outings he scored 15 goals, a modest return for a forward with one of Scotland's giants. Yet Donnelly's qualities range far beyond simply goalscoring. Mobility, pace and an unquenchable spirit are high among the Glasgow-born Donnelly's assets which have attracted Scotland coach Craig Brown's attention.

'Simon has flair and is one of the brightest young talents in Scottish football,' said Brown, who has monitored Donnelly's progress in the Scottish Under-21 ranks. Donnelly first sprung to prominence in the Toulon Under-21 tournament, when he scored on his debut at that level in June 1994.

But the man who groomed Donnelly for a Scotland future warned his former prodigy that he still has some way to go before he deserves hero status. 'He's proved nothing yet,' said Eddie Hunter, who coached Donnelly for six months at Queens Park. 'The way the game is now, anyone who looks busy on the field can look a good player.

'We worked hard on Donnelly's touch and runs for six months and I'm pleased the way things are going for him.'

Donnelly was playing in the youth and reserve teams at Queens Park when Celtic manager Liam Brady asked to take him on a youth tournament visit to Switzerland. 'When they wanted to sign him afterwards we couldn't stand in his way,' added Hunter.

He came to the attention of English clubs in September last year with outstanding UEFA Cup performances against Liverpool, broadcast live on television north and south of the border. Now he awaits a further chance to prove he can competently handle the big occasion – and they don't come much bigger than the World Cup.

Gordon Durie

Club: Rangers
Previous clubs: East Fife, Hibernian, Chelsea, Tottenham
Height: 6'0"
Born: 6 December 1965
International debut: v Bulgaria 1-0
(Sofia) 11 November 1987

'I love playing for Scotland and I'm grateful I can play in several positions.'

Gordon Durie has been Scotland's Mr Durable for a decade, winning 38 caps mainly as a striker alongside several different partners. France '98 could be the final major international stage for Durie to display his talents. Though not a prolific scorer, Durie's pace and vision have created many a goal-scoring opportunity for Scotland and his various clubs.

Two London outfits valued Durie's talents so highly that they were persuaded to pay record fees. It

is all a far cry from those tentative early days of Durie's career, as a central defender in school and youth football with the Hill of Beath Hawthorn club. He joined East Fife at 14 and was playing in the Scottish Second Division at 16. Durie proved his pedigree in Scotland, scoring 41 goals in 121 games and becoming something of a legend with Hibernian, where he established his reputation either as a bustling central striker or a fleet-footed winger.

He then moved south to Chelsea for a club record £381,000 fee in April 1986 where he became a firm favourite with the Stamford Bridge fans. His performances there first brought Durie to the attention of Scotland, which soon launched his long international career by calling him up for the Under-21 side. The man they call 'Jukebox' has had defenders dancing to his tune ever since. Tottenham also paid a club record

fee for Durie when they forked out £2.2 million to Chelsea in August 1991 in order to partner him with England's Gary Lineker.

The pair were nicknamed the 'G-force' as their goals took Tottenham to the quarter-finals of the European Cup Winners' Cup. Durie fell out with the club over a fine of two weeks' wages for swearing at manager Ossie Ardiles – just weeks after winning his appeal to the FA over a misconduct charge when he was accused of feigning injury in a headtohead encounter with Coventry defender Andy Pearce. Paisley-born Durie 'came home' in November 1993 when Rangers paid Tottenham £1 million for him.

Durie has admitted his last five weeks at White Hart Lane were a nightmare, but it ended with a dream move which relaunched his ailing career at the age of 27. His Scotland place, surrendered during the dispute with Tottenham, was soon regained and Durie has never looked back.

He is a key figure behind Rangers' latest bid for honours and with Duncan Ferguson opting out of the international scene, Durie's previous experience of European and World Cup campaigns is certain to make him a vital figure in France at the age of 32.

Matt Elliott

Club: Leicester City
Previous clubs: Charlton Athletic, Torquay United,
    Scunthorpe United, Oxford United
Height: 6'3"
Born: 1 November 1968
International debut: v France 1-2
    (St Étienne) 12 November 1997

'I thought the chance to play at this level had passed me by.'

When Matt Elliott rejected the opportunity to play professional football as a youngster – opting instead to work on a building site – he could little have dreamed he would end up going to the World Cup finals with Scotland.

The Wandsworth-born centre-half has certainly come a long way since turning down Crystal Palace's invitation to sign schoolboy forms with the club. But the 29-year-old is now firmly in the frame with Craig Brown, courtesy of an Edinburgh-born grandmother.

Described by Brown as a 'colossus', Elliott has blossomed late in the game, but since joining Leicester from Oxford United in January 1997 for £1.6 million, he has firmly established himself as one of the most accomplished defenders in the Premiership and his Scotland call-up against France was no more than his impressive performances deserved.

Elliott learnt his trade the hard way, languishing in the lower leagues with Torquay, Scunthorpe and Oxford United for some eight seasons before Leicester manager Martin O'Neill decided he was ready for the big-time. He took to the challenge like a duck to water. Passionate and committed to a fault, Elliott is a genuinely rounded player who is equally comfortable dealing with an aerial bombardment at the heart of the defence or popping up in the opposition box, often to devastating effect. In his first season with Leicester he averaged a goal every four Premiership matches, and was unlucky to miss out on the Foxes' triumphant Coca-Cola Cup run because he was cup-tied.

Like Arsenal's Ian Wright, he is now making up for lost time and Scotland is the main beneficiary. He said: 'I think players who come the long way up appreciate it. At the end of my career I want to have no regrets, to have achieved what I can and enjoyed it whatever happens.'

Although he lacks real pace, his reading of the game means he is seldom exposed by opposition strikers and his timing of tackles is reminiscent of team-mate Colin Hendry. France '98 is Elliott's first and probably last chance to make a name for himself on the international stage and, if his form for Leicester is any guide, he should have few worries about doing so.

Kevin Gallacher

Club: Blackburn Rovers
Previous clubs: Dundee United, Coventry City
Height: 5'8"
Born: 23 November 1966
International debut: v Colombia 0-0
(Glasgow) 17 May 1988

'If anyone wants to know about broken legs, see an expert. Come to me!'

In a side which has often been criticized for its lack of goals, Kevin Gallacher may well be the exception. And this particular striker is no goal-hanger; the six goals he scored in World Cup qualification were by no means his only contribution to the noble cause.

The big question asked at Blackburn last season was whether Chris Sutton had done enough to deserve a place in the England squad. But those inside Ewood Park and beyond seemed to forget that one Rovers striker had already booked his ticket to France.

Last year Kevin Gallacher moved from bit-player to leading light on the domestic and international scenes, his partnership with Sutton leading to a glut of goals in the Premiership, and his double-act with Gordon Durie attracting plaudits on the bigger stage. Rovers manager Roy Hodgson had no hesitation in offering him an extension to his contract, knowing as well as anyone in the stands that Gallacher was hitting the form of his life. Now, at the age of 31, he has never been so valuable.

Three years ago the story was rather different. Blackburn may have been celebrating its first Championship in 81 years, but there was no medal for Kevin Gallacher. He had been kept out of first-team action for 15 months

with a double leg fracture when he made his return on 22 April 1995. Crystal Palace were the opponents, and three points were the target as the club moved ever closer to that elusive title. The fairy-tale return seemed to have been written when Gallacher scored the

winning goal, but the story was not complete. Gallacher did not finish that game – he had broken his leg for the second time.

But Gallacher is a born footballer and returned fitter, faster and far more determined than ever. He comes from a family of footballers: both his grandfather Patsy and uncle William turned out for Celtic. Another uncle, Tommy, played for Dundee. Kevin followed in Uncle Tommy's footsteps, and began his career with the Tannadice club. In 1990 he moved south to Coventry, a transition which seemed to lose him his place in the 1990 World Cup squad.

There is little danger of that happening again this year. Not even a move to Highfield Road could convince Craig Brown that Gallacher is not the man to lead Scotland's attack in France.

Scot Gemmill

Club: Nottingham Forest
Previous clubs: none
Height: 5'11"
Born: 2 January 1971
International debut: v Japan 0-0
(Hiroshima) 21 May 1995

'Craig Brown knows I'll never let him down.'

His father Archie Gemmill scored one of the most memorable goals in Scotland's World Cup history, but son Scot admits he doesn't get too much advice from dad.

'Before the qualifier against Belarus he was about as vocal as he gets,' reveals Scot. 'He told me to enjoy the game and to take my chance if I get it. But that's only because I was giving him a lift to the airport!'

Archie's stunning strike in Argentina in 1978 helped Scotland to a 3-2 victory over Holland, but it wasn't enough to keep them in the competition. Now Gemmill junior has a chance to make his mark on the world stage.

A regular Scotland squad member throughout both Euro '96 and the World Cup qualifying campaign, Gemmill has been less fortunate domestically, suffering relegation with Nottingham Forest in 1997 and losing his first-team place along the way. However, he battled his way back into the team, becoming nearly ever-present this season, and Craig Brown has shown faith with him over the years. But Gemmill admitted: 'When you are out of the team, of course it is a worry.

The longer you're out the more pressure there is on Craig Brown to drop you. But he knows I'll never let him down. I'd like to think the way I played for Scotland when asked kept me in the squad when I was out of Forest's first team.

'But I've been out of the Forest team before and then re-established my place. I always work hard.' This is a principle that Gemmill has stuck to since he began his professional career at the age of 17, when Brian Clough signed the youngster.

'Having a famous dad certainly helped,' admits Scot, 'because his friendship with Mr Clough got me a contract. I just wasn't good enough at the time and nobody would have predicted that I would go on to play for Scotland. But I worked and improved.'

It's a dedication that has won the respect of Archie, who confirms: 'It would be silly to say I didn't have an influence on Scot in the early days, but his subsequent success is down to him. From 18 onwards he's done it his way. The old man was very definitely put in his place!'

Andy Goram

Club: Rangers
Previous clubs: Oldham Athletic, Hibernian
Height: 5'11"
Born: 13 September 1964
International debut: v East Germany 0-0 (Glasgow) 16 October 1985

'The bigger the game, the more enjoyment I get. Excitement is what football is all about but if it wasn't for my wife I'd be an 18-stone alcoholic bricklayer playing for Penicuik Athletic – assuming they could find a jersey to fit me.'

A notoriously bad loser, Andy Goram, the Rangers goalkeeper, chose the right club when he moved from Hibernian in 1991, replacing then England international Chris Woods. The Scotland goalkeeper has since played a massive role in Ibrox's domestic domination, which has reaped six championships, three Scottish Cups and three Scottish League Cups.

But his career has been followed by controversy and it is testament to his talents that he has bounced back time and again. In 1995 he walked out on the Scotland squad claiming he was not 'mentally attuned' for a European Championship qualifier. He was then put on the transfer list for a short while by Rangers manager Walter Smith, because of a poor attitude to training.

With an eye for a flutter and a publicly unstable home life, Goram courted more controversy when he turned out for his international cricket team. He was actually registered as a batsman for four years with Lancashire but when he had to make the choice, football was the winner.

Since committing himself to Rangers in 1994 Goram has gone from strength to strength. But it could so easily have been England that he represented. A native of Bury in Lancashire, Goram was included in the England Under-21 squad by manager Howard Wilkinson but never played a game. He was released by West Bromwich Albion after serving his apprenticeship, a decision which the Midlands club must have regretted a thousand times since. Just a couple of years later when he was only 21 he was included in the same Scotland squad as Alan Rough and Jim Leighton.

Oldham chief Joe Royle recommended his keeper to Scotland manager Alex Ferguson; and it was not long before he earned his first full cap. He qualifies for the team through his father Lew, who also wore the No. 1 shirt for Hibs and Bury.

With a reputation as an excellent shot-stopper and with the ability to pluck the ball out of the air with ease, the former Oldham keeper has won nearly 50 caps.

Colin Hendry

Club: Blackburn Rovers
Previous clubs: Dundee, Blackburn, Manchester City
Height: 6'1"
Born: 7 December 1965
International debut: v Estonia 3-0
(Tallinn) 19 May 1993

'The more fortunate and successful you become, the easier things come to you.'

If there is one player who epitomizes the Braveheart spirit of the Scotland side above all others, it is Colin Hendry, whose ruddy cheeks and wild-flowing blond locks betray the battling nature of the man.

The 32-year-old Blackburn defender inspired his club to the English Premiership title in 1994-95 with a never-say-die attitude that overcomes any supposed deficiencies in technique and pace. Hendry bestrides any defence he plays in like a colossus. When the boots and the elbows start flying, Hendry dives in where others fear to tread, a towering example to team-mates, an inspiring sight to supporters.

It was not always so. His early career took in Dundee, an unremarkable first spell at Ewood Park and two frustrating years in an under-achieving Manchester City side. The moment that transformed Hendry's footballing life and set him on the road to

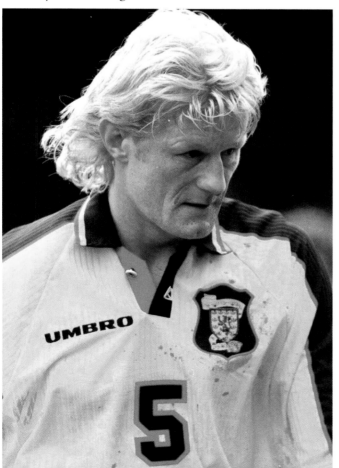

France '98 arrived in October 1991, when Kenny Dalglish took over the managerial reins at Blackburn, then in the English Second Division. Within a month Dalglish brought Hendry back to Ewood Park for £700,000 and the rock of Rovers' success was founded.

Hendry's first international call came at the comparatively late age of 27, in the less than auspicious surroundings of the Tallinn stadium in Estonia. But such is his strength and dependability, not to mention a domineering heading ability, that the Keith-born defender quickly established himself under new Scotland coach, Craig Brown.

Hendry's comparatively meagre total of 28 caps does not adequately reflect his importance to the Scotland team. Those appearances include the Euro '96 tournament and Hendry's most embarrassing moment on the international scene. It came in the 2-0 defeat by hosts England at Wembley, when Paul Gascoigne lobbed and left him sitting on his backside before

scoring England's second goal. It is a measure of Hendry's unflappability that such moments stand out by their rarity. Far more common is the sight of Hendry thundering forward to add his power to Scotland's attack at set-pieces. Surprisingly, his only international goal to date was Scotland's second in its 2-0 win in Malta in November 1993 – Craig Brown's first match in charge.

The World Cup represents Hendry's final opportunity of performing on the greatest stage of all. With the relish typical of one for whom success has come late in his career, he is determined to leave his own distinctive mark.

David Hopkin

Club: Leeds United
Previous clubs: Morton, Chelsea, Crystal Palace
Height: 5'9"
Born: 21 August 1970
International debut: v Malta 3-2
(Valletta) 1 June 1997

'We are both Scottish and both play in midfield, but the only real reason I'm compared to Billy [Bremner] is that we both have ginger hair.'

David Hopkin's ability to score spectacular goals made him an instant hit with the Tartan Army. His double-strike against Belarus in a World Cup qualifier, after coming on as a substitute, sealed a vital victory and made Hopkin's gap-toothed grin as famous north of the border as it was in England.

A latecomer to top-flight football, Hopkin announced himself to the football world at large with a brilliant last-minute curling strike that gave Crystal Palace victory over Sheffield United in last season's First Division play-off final. Having guided Palace to the Premiership, Hopkin flew the Eagles nest and moved to Leeds in the close season for £3.25 million. George Graham confirmed his faith in his fellow Scot by making him club captain. Graham's decision

completed a remarkable transformation for Hopkin, who just a few years earlier was struggling to get into first-team football. The problem was not lack of ability, but rather an excess of versatility that left managers unsure where to play him.

At Chelsea, under future England boss Glenn Hoddle, Hopkin languished in the reserves, falling into the dreaded category of 'utility player' and unable to make any one position his own. With time marching on, Hopkin took the risk of dropping down a division and joined Palace. Manager Steve Coppell put Hopkin in centre-midfield. Hopkin repaid his manager's faith in him by scoring 13 League goals in Palace's promotion campaign, making him the club's second topscorer.

All the while his skills were drawing admiring looks far beyond the confines of South London and it was no surprise to anyone when Hopkin left for Leeds. Graham, not known for wasting money in the transfer market, has had his judgment vindicated once again, with Hopkin a major factor in Leeds' revival.

Before last summer, Scotland's midfield trio of Gary McAllister, John Collins and Paul Lambert looked to be certain of their starting places, but McAllister's injury and Hopkin's performances have changed all that and left Craig Brown thankful for the extra option.

As for Hopkin, a late-developer he may be, but few have worked harder to make up for lost time. What price him producing a curler to match his Wembley effort in the opener against Brazil?

Darren Jackson

Club: Celtic
Previous clubs: Meadowbank Thistle, Newcastle United, Dundee United, Hibernian
Height: 5'10"
Born: 25 July 1966
International debut: v Russia 0-0 (Moscow) 29 March 1995

'I want to be remembered as the guy who scored goals for Scotland and not the player who had a brain operation to save his career.'

Last August Darren Jackson would not have predicted that he would be in France for the World Cup finals this year. He would probably have been happy to think that he would be cheering on his former team-mates from the comfort of his Scottish home. For just months after a £1.25 million dream move to Celtic, Jackson was diagnosed as having a brain disorder. It not only seemed likely to end his career, but also threatened to end his life. By November, however, Jackson had proved the medics wrong, appearing as a substitute in the Old Firm game. The standing ovation he received was not restricted to the Celtic section of the ground. Even die-hard Rangers fans had to applaud this man's bravery.

Jackson believes that he has come back as a player even better than the one who went into the operating room. Craig Brown clearly agrees, making it obvious from the outset that his place in the Scotland squad was waiting for him alongside hundreds of cards from well-wishers.

Jackson's professional career began in 1985, when Meadowbank Thistle plucked him from the obscurity of Broxburn Amateurs. One season later and 17 goals to the good, Newcastle United raised him from Meadowbank obscurity into the full limelight.

But Jackson had left his shooting boots behind in Scotland, and in 1989 Dundee United brought him home after a disappointing spell in England. He soon regained his form, and averaged 12 League goals a season over three years with the club.

A move to Hibs followed, and in 1995 the call-up came to the Scotland side. Jackson is the first to admit that he was not a popular choice, but once he had broken his scoring duck against Latvia in the autumn of 1996 his popularity increased at the same rate as his footballing stature.

A year ago he proved he had the nerve for the big occasion, when he converted two penalties to keep Hibs in the top flight. But it would be his final performance for the Edinburgh club, as Celtic beckoned. Coach Wim Jansen was persuaded to part with £1.25 million on the strength of seeing videos of Jackson's performances for Scotland. That should convince any detractors that Jackson is worth his place in the line-up.

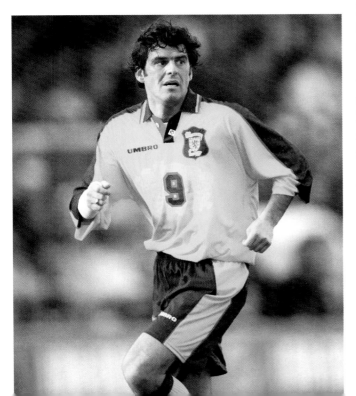

Eoin Jess

Club: Aberdeen
Previous clubs: Aberdeen, Coventry
Height: 5'9"
Born: 13 December 1970
International debut: v Italy 0-3
          (Rome) 18 November 1992

'After I heard I was left out of the squad for America, I had written off my chances for England – you just don't think something like this will happen.'

Eoin Jess, although slightly built, is probably one of the fastest forwards in Scottish football. With excellent ball-control, he is very difficult to catch. An impressive striking partner for Billy Dodds at Aberdeen, Jess is equally at home as an attacking midfielder just behind the front two.

Jess left Aberdeen in February 1996 for Coventry but was unable to settle and took his time getting into

the struggling Midlands side. His form picked up in the closing stages of the 1996-97 season, though, and he scored the winning goal against QPR, dooming them to relegation and saving Coventry. He rejoined Aberdeen for £750,000 in July 1997, just in time for the new season. A huge favourite of the Pittodrie fans, his talents are now in full bloom again, with a steady scoring record exemplified by his two goals against Motherwell in December 1997. These showed his ability to unnerve the opposition with lightning runs and raking passes.

His constant flashes of brilliance in the otherwise lacklustre Aberdeen side this season have earned him a deserved recall to the national side, and Jess is certainly playing as well as any Scottish forward at the moment. He has dash, imagination and class, all of which will be much needed to cope with Scotland's difficult group in the World Cup.

As one of the brightest stars to emerge from the Scottish game for some years, Jess won international recognition at the age of 21, during his first period with Aberdeen. His only goal for Scotland so far came in the 5-0 drubbing of the hapless San Marino late in 1995 in a Euro '96 qualifying game. Scotland had already qualified by then and Jess was recalled to play up front with Scott Booth. Scotland had been finding it hard to score goals, but Jess gave them inspiration with the opener in the 30th minute. He had already made three unsuccessful attempts on goal before receiving the telling pass from Pat Nevin. The Aberdeen duo of Jess and Booth cut the San Marino defence to pieces, forcing countless errors and creating dozens of chances.

Craig Brown had not intended to use Jess for the Euro '96 competition itself the following summer, but had to think again after Paul McStay dropped out with an ankle injury. In Scotland's warm-up tour of America before the championship in England, Jess made the starting line-up against the USA and was brought on as a late substitute for John Spencer against Colombia. He made the subs bench when Scotland faced England at Wembley in June and now, at 28, he may have his final chance to perform for his country on the world stage.

Paul Lambert

Club: Celtic
Previous clubs: St Mirren, Motherwell, Borussia Dortmund
Height: 5'11'
Born: 7 August 1969
International debut: v Japan 0-0
(Hiroshima) 21 May 1995

'It would be a wonderful honour to play in France, but I don't want to go there and just be content to get knocked out early on.'

There are few Scots who can claim to have won a European winner's medal in recent years, but one man who can boast such an achievement is Paul Lambert – the man German legend Andreas Möller has described as one of the greatest players to come out of Scotland. But back in 1996 when his contract at Motherwell expired, there were few clubs on the phone to his agent vying for his services. He

had already been capped by Scotland, but Paul Lambert was not a name that excited managers or fans.

The one club who thought that a free transfer under the Bosman Ruling was a bargain were German champions Borussia Dortmund. It was a curious transition from a Scottish relegation battle to a European Cup campaign, but it was a transition which Lambert made willingly and with ease. It was only when Borussia Dortmund played Manchester United, and Lambert and his colleagues successfully stifled the United midfield, that news of Lambert's success reached home. And then when Dortmund won the European Cup, with a rousing display against Juventus, the offers began to come in from the clubs who had not wanted to know a year earlier.

Last November Lambert agreed to a £1.7 million move to Celtic, his family's welfare figuring high in his decision to return to Scotland. Lambert's departure was an emotional one – he retired from the Westfalenstadion in tears.

Although the form that had been with him in Germany did not immediately show at Celtic Park, any early problems settling in were forgotten when he scored his first goal for the Bhoys – against Old Firm rivals Rangers. This was guaranteed to win him immediate legend status at Celtic, and even his Rangers-mad father had to applaud.

Coca-Cola Cup success came in his first season with Celtic, making him undoubtedly the first player to have won three different cups with St. Mirren, Borussia Dortmund and Celtic. The first medal had come at the age of 17, when he was part of Saints' historic Scottish Cup-winning side. And with Lambert's record in cup competitions, Craig Brown would be unwise to leave him out of his World Cup line-up.

Jim Leighton

Club: Hibernian
Previous clubs: Aberdeen, Manchester United, Reading (loan), Dundee, Sheffield United (loan)
Height: 6'1"
Born: 24 July 1958
International debut: v East Germany 2-0 (Glasgow) 13 October 1982

'Any goalkeeper who ends up with his legs round his shoulders won't get much respect from me. If you can make a save look easy it takes a bit of heart out of a forward.'

Jim Leighton and Scottish goalkeeper are words which are inextricably linked in most people's minds. But only Kenny Dalglish has pulled on a Scotland shirt more times than Leighton, and that is not bad company for anybody to find himself in.

Five years ago, however, Leighton considered

retiring from the game, and only after reassurances from family and friends that he did have a future in football did Leighton concede to try again. He had been rejected by Manchester United, and the promising escape route to Dundee had proved to be a jump from the frying-pan into a much less comfortable fire. But Hibs manager Alex Miller believed in him, and took him on a free transfer – almost certainly the best money that he never had to spend.

Leighton has never looked back, grabbing his second chance with the same enthusiasm with which he grabbed his first, a move out of the Department of Employment and into professional football with Aberdeen. He had been a Rangers fanatic as a boy but the Dons would certainly do. That was 20 years ago, Leighton making the move to Pittodrie on the recommendation of former Danish international goalkeeper Erik Sorensen. Aberdeen manager Alex Ferguson soon became another famous fan, once describing Leighton as 'possibly the best goalkeeper in Europe'. This was quite an accolade from one of the world's finest judges of footballing talent to a shot-stopper. Ferguson and Leighton formed a formidable partnership, and together won every honour in the Scottish game, as well as the European Cup Winners' Cup.

When Ferguson was appointed manager of Manchester United it was inevitable that Leighton would not be long in following and in 1988 he was unveiled as the club's new £750,000 signing. Two years later the friendship and mutual respect that had made that move inevitable were dissolved when Ferguson left Leighton out of the side for a FA Cup Final replay. He dropped from automatic first choice, to a disappointed second choice and eventually to third choice keeper at United. As a result he lost his place in the Scotland line-up, and that seemed to be the beginning of the end for Leighton.

But the Johnstone-born keeper was made of sterner stuff, and the form he boasts now is such that Craig Brown has a very difficult job not picking him. And if Jim Leighton has his way, it will be Dalglish who will trail him in the Scotland annals.

Ally McCoist

Club: Rangers
Previous clubs: St Johnstone, Sunderland
Height: 5'10"
Born: 24 September 1962
International debut: v Holland 0-0
(Eindhoven) 29 April 1986

'People ask why Scotland have trouble scoring. The truth is the majority of teams attack harder than we do.'

Ally McCoist has been around the Scotland scene for over a decade and it is a tribute to his stamina that he comes into the World Cup reckoning at the age of 35.

McCoist has so many careers these days he must have needed the services of a personal financial adviser to help with his self-assessment tax forms. He established himself as a television personality with his wise-cracking appearances as a team captain on the BBC quiz show *A Question of Sport*. McCoist is also a successful racehorse owner, quite apart from his day job as striker with Glasgow Rangers. McCoist won his 58th Scotland cap as a substitute in a World Cup qualifier against Belarus in September, but was not even on the bench for the next two internationals.

He earned immortality among Rangers supporters by breaking the club's 57-year-old scoring record with a goal against Raith that took his total to 231 – one better than Bob McPhail in 1939. His golden years at the club include a 39-goal season and McCoist himself insists his best years were those when he partnered Mark Hateley. The pair claimed 140 goals between them in two seasons.

His career, however, was slow to gain initial momentum. McCoist made his League debut for St Johnstone in a 3-0 victory over Raith Rovers in April 1979. He failed to score for the club in 19 League outings over two seasons but in the third he made scouts all over Scotland sit up with 22 goals in 38 League outings. Rangers manager John Greig offered a club record £350,000 for McCoist, who was keener to try his luck in England and joined Sunderland for the same amount. But the move came too soon; McCoist couldn't settle and after scoring just eight times in 56 League games, spread over two seasons, Sunderland decided they could manage without him.

'I was young and had a great deal to learn,' said McCoist. 'It was very sound experience for me. If I could turn back the clock and have the same choices I would do the same thing again.'

Sunderland's loss was Rangers' gain as they snapped him up for less than half the amount Greig had offered. He was Rangers' leading scorer in eight of his first nine seasons there, finishing runner-up to Mo Johnston at the end of the 1990-91 season because manager Graeme Souness chose Johnston and Hateley ahead of him.

Billy McKinlay

Club: Blackburn Rovers
Previous clubs: Dundee United
Height: 5'8"
Born: 22 April 1969
International debut: v Malta 2-0
(Valletta) 17 November 1993

'If we can't get our minds right for this challenge, then we shouldn't be here.'

Talk about Scottish internationals at Ewood Park tends to centre around Kevin Gallacher's goalscoring exploits for club and country or Colin Hendry's fiercely competitive performances at the back. Yet it's not beyond the bounds of possibility that, come the start of France '98, Hendry and Gallacher will be lining up alongside another Blackburn player, Billy McKinlay.

McKinlay is the sort of player who rarely makes newspaper headlines, although he generated a fair deal of copy north of the border following his acrimonious departure from Dundee United. He joined Blackburn in 1995 for £1.75 million, having eventually decided against taking United to court over the legality of an eight-and-a-half-year contract he signed as a youngster. When he came south to Ewood, Blackburn were looking nothing like the side that had won the Championship the previous season. But McKinlay was one of the players who helped steady nerves and he performed creditably.

Although once memorably described, after a disappointing performance against Sweden, as being as 'disorientated as a man plunged into a new profession,' McKinlay is nothing if not a battler.

Far more important to him than the assessment of a journalist was the opinion of Blackburn manager Roy Hodgson. In November McKinlay signed a new three-and-a-half-year contract, reportedly making him one of the top ten highest paid players in Britain.

He would have been out of contract this summer, but Roy Hodgson was not going to wait for the effects of the Bosman Ruling to kick-in. The new deal was a deserved reward for McKinlay's efforts in playing a key role for Rovers last season as the Lancashire club clawed its way out of the relegation zone.

McKinlay is quick to credit Hodgson as the man who has helped him revitalize his career. 'Our manager has brought a lot of new ideas from Italy to Blackburn and it paid off with a superb start to the season. He has got us believing that we can win trophies again and both Kevin and I have had our confidence boosted.'

In common with many of his team-mates, this could be McKinlay's last chance for international glory and Scotland will need his midfield skills to be at their peak if they are to go into the second round.

Tosh McKinlay

Club: Celtic
Previous clubs: Dundee, Hearts
Height: 5'10"
Born: 3 December 1964
International debut: v Greece 1-0
(Glasgow) 16 August 1995

'It was a great day when Scotland qualified for the World Cup and it means a great deal to me that I've played a part in achieving that.'

Tosh McKinlay is used to battling against the odds. The fierce-tackling full-back deserves everything he has gained from football on his way to fulfilling his boyhood dreams. His fierce determination can be gauged from the seemingly boundless energy that fuels the trademark driving runs through midfield, turning defence into attack in an instant.

McKinlay is the sort of man you would want alongside you in the trenches – a quality recognized by Craig Brown and by the Celtic Park faithful who accepted him readily when he joined his idols from Hearts in November 1994 for the bargain fee of £350,000.

Success has come late to the full-back. Born in Glasgow, he began his career with Dundee, but it was with Hearts that he first rose to prominence. McKinlay's own heart lay away from Tynecastle, however, and when the opportunity presented itself to return to Glasgow, McKinlay found the lure impossible to resist. Virtually ever-present during Tommy Burns' reign at Parkhead, McKinlay became that rarity among footballers – an international whose debut came after his 30th birthday.

Called-up by Brown to bolster his injury-hit squad in facing Greece in a crucial European Championship qualifier at Hampden Park, McKinlay started the match. He made such a lasting impression on Brown in the 1-0 victory, which virtually sealed their passage to the finals tournament in England, that the coach now hands him the No.3 jersey as a matter of routine. How bitter a pill to swallow then, when new Celtic coach, Dutchman Wim Jansen decided the destiny of one of Scotland's oldest clubs lay in the hands of foreign players. Having made 103 appearances for the Bhoys, McKinlay found himself frozen out of Jansen's plans, with Frenchman Stephane Mahe assuming his place in the side.

Despite his popularity among the Celtic faithful, McKinlay had to consider his burning ambition to play in the World Cup. It wasn't going to happen for him as long as he remained in Celtic's reserve team, so at the age of 33, he headed south to Stoke on a loan deal. McKinlay's new career didn't start too promisingly, however. Sent off on his debut, a 2-1 home defeat by Middlesbrough, the Scot with the big heart does not give up.

John Spencer

Club: Queens Park Rangers
Previous clubs: Glasgow Rangers, Morton, Chelsea
Height: 5'6"
Born: 11 September 1970
International debut: v Russia 1-1
 (Glasgow) 16 November 1994

'You have to be confident and aggressive. If you're shy and retiring in football, you'll get trampled on.'

What John Spencer lacks in stature, he makes up for in the speed of his feet and his razor-sharp mind. The diminutive striker's great asset is a mobility which keeps even the most agile of international defences on their guard. Yet few of the Scotland squad will have made as many sacrifices as Spencer to realize their World Cup ambitions.

Brought up on the tough Gorbals estates in Glasgow, he was stymied by the quality of the forwards who surrounded him at his first club Rangers, and was forced to broaden his horizons in search of first-team football. To England, in fact, and Chelsea.

The relatively untried youngster arrived

at Stamford Bridge in August 1992 with a hefty £450,000 price-tag hanging around his neck. It didn't take long for the Chelsea fans to respond to Spencer's all-action, bustling style. With 36 goals in 103 appearances for the club, 28 as substitute, Spencer played a significant role in establishing Chelsea's cup pedigree under Glenn Hoddle.

He was a member of the side which lost to Manchester United in the 1994 FA Cup Final and then scored a memorable length-of-the-pitch solo goal against Austria Vienna in the following season's European Cup Winners' Cup run to the semi-finals.

When Ruud Gullit took over as Chelsea manager, Spencer found himself behind Mark Hughes and Gianluca Vialli in the pecking order. The arrival of Gianfranco Zola from Parma, in November 1996 proved to be the last straw for him. He could foresee his first-team opportunities being limited.

Again he moved, realizing that out of sight, out of Craig Brown's mind, was no place to be if he was going to force his way back into the Scotland squad. Just a week after welcoming Zola to Stamford Bridge, Spencer decided for the sake of his international career and the enticing carrot of France '98 to drop down into the Nationwide League First Division by joining Queens Park Rangers. He soon justified the £2.5 million fee by notching up 17 goals in 25 games last season and established himself as a favourite with the fans.

Spencer has an enviable record on the international scene, having represented Scotland at every level from schoolboy to the full side. His 14 caps have included seven as substitute, although there would surely have been more already if he had been able to break his scoring duck for Scotland.

Neil Sullivan

Club: Wimbledon
Previous clubs: Crystal Palace (loan)
Height: 6'0"
Born: 24 February 1970
International debut: v Wales 0-1
(Kilmarnock) 27 May 1997

'No matter how much you study, how hard you train or how well you prepare, fate can take a hand.'

Neil Sullivan's first brush with fame as Wimbledon's goalkeeper was not exactly ideal. He was in goal when Manchester United's David Beckham scored *that* goal from the halfway line on the opening day of the 1996–97 season.

Four days later he let in almost as spectacular a goal against Newcastle, when David Batty scored from long range. A rocket of a shot from Lee Sharpe in the next game simply added to the attention surrounding Sullivan, for all the wrong reasons. It speaks volumes for Sullivan's subsequent performances that he was to earn his first cap at the end of that season with less than 100 first-team games to his name. He claims there was little he could do about Beckham's shot but has acknowledged that rather than hinder his career, it actually helped him. It was through a subsequent magazine article about the goal that Craig Brown discovered Sullivan's eligibility for the Scots. He qualifies for Scotland through a grandparent and has refuted accusations that he should not represent his country through such a distant link.

A solid performance against Wales on his debut is likely to be the first of many caps for the young man from Malden in South London. Sullivan must take some credit for helping Wimbledon go on a 19-game unbeaten run in the 1996-97 season, taking his team into European contention and the semi-finals of the FA and Coca-Cola Cups.

The Manchester United game was finally laid to rest in the FA Cup fourth-round replay against the champions, when a superb save denied Gary Pallister and secured the Dons' place in the next round. Despite helping Wimbledon to a run of only three defeats in 31 games, Sullivan and his club ended last season without a trophy or a European place.

Sullivan started watching the Dons at Plough Lane as a youngster and joined them at the age of 11. The 1996-97 season was his first as the undisputed No. 1 after a patient apprenticeship behind Dave Beasant and Hans Segers. Twice he forced his way into the first team after battling back from broken legs, and with Alex Ferguson as one of his biggest fans, Sullivan has admiration from the very best.

David Weir

Club: Hearts
Previous clubs: Falkirk
Height: 6'3"
Born: 10 May 1970
International debut: v Wales 0-1 (Kilmarnock) 27 May 1997

'It's great to be involved with Scotland. I'm going to work at my game and take it from there.'

Weir is one of the so-called 'fringe' players in Craig Brown's World Cup squad, a challenger to the likes of Hendry, Calderwood and Elliott for a role in the centre of Scotland's defence. A highly-rated central defender who was exciting the interest of the likes of Liverpool and Rangers, he eventually elected to move to Hearts in 1996, the 27-year-old fits the classic centre-half mould. He is strong, towering, able in the air and never unnecessarily flamboyant. Weir is also particularly dangerous attacking from set pieces, an attribute that has seen him score some important goals for Hearts.

Scottish champions Rangers tabled a £1 million bid for Weir which fell through and Hearts boss Jim Jeffries scooped him up from his previous club, Falkirk, for a bargain £250,000. In his first season at Tynecastle, Weir put in a series of excellent performances and scored some vital goals. As a result he was nominated by his fellow pros for Player of the Year and that's when he began to catch the eye of Craig Brown.

The giant Hearts stopper was first called to international duty relatively late in his career, in May 1997. He was informed of his call-up as he made his way to Majorca on a club holiday.

'I'm absolutely thrilled to be part of the squad. I've enjoyed my first season with Hearts and this is the icing on the cake for me,' declared a delighted Weir.

Weir has made a notable contribution to the three games which he has played for his country, friendlies against Wales, Malta and a World Cup warm-up against France in St-Étienne. Against the World Cup hosts, Weir proved more than a match for the aggressive Bordeaux striker, Lilian Laslandes and is aware that next up could be Rámario or Ronaldo.

'It was a really testing match which I thoroughly enjoyed. I was pleased with my display but really I thought everyone contributed,' said Weir. 'It was nice to hear the Scottish voices in the crowd – our fans once again made themselves heard.'

As club captain, Weir has been the backbone of the Hearts revival this season, which has seen the Jambos pose a real threat to the Old Firm dominance of the Scottish League and given them hope for its first trophy in 35 years. The Scotland stopper missed a couple of weeks (less than expected) in February when he went into hospital for surgery to correct a niggling knee injury.

The High Road to France

Craig Brown didn't have many problems spotting the potholes when the qualifying draw mapped out Scotland's route to France: the names Austria and Sweden loomed large; the rest of the six-table group was made up of those new states of fractured Europe, Latvia, Estonia and Belarus, all with the potential to upset the odds.

Yet the focus was on Austria – first port of call for a Scotland side that has a fine World Cup qualifying tradition, stained slightly by the failure to make it through to America in 1994. That miss ended a remarkable run – not emulated by the auld enemy south of the border – of five successive World Cup finals appearances.

And so to Vienna at the end of August 1996. Sweden had already put down their marker with a tidy 5-1 demolition of Belarus two months earlier and for both Scotland and Austria it was vital to kick-off cautiously – start on the wrong foot and it is virtually impossible to get back on the right one.

Tense, as these matches always are, it was Scotland who carved out the better chances – and wasted them. The chief culprit was Duncan Ferguson, the Everton striker, who was to play in just two of the ten qualifying matches and then announce his retirement from international football.

Meanwhile, a 2-1 win for Sweden in Latvia meant that the Scandinavians were still setting the pace and it was essential for Scotland to bag a win in Latvia. They did – and in style. First John Collins, the former

Celtic and Hibs player now with Monaco, smashed home a free-kick and then Hibs' Darren Jackson scored his first international goal. Any hopes of building on that win – Estonia was the next port of call three days later – were wrecked by a farce of Brian Rix proportions.

The Scotland team were lined up, the referee blew his whistle, the ball was played forward by Billy Dodds to Collins and the referee Miroslav Radoman blew his whistle to end the match. Estonia, with a training camp 60 miles away, had failed to show after FIFA had ordered that the game be brought forward for an earlier kick-off because of fears that the ground's floodlights were not up to scratch. Scotland departed thinking that they would be awarded the game – by a standard 3-0 margin – and with it the points. Instead a replay was ordered on a neutral ground.

Meanwhile, Austria had pricked the Sweden bubble by winning away and really hit their stride with a 2-1 home win over Latvia – all of which increased the pressure on Scotland for the Ibrox visit of Sweden in November 1996.

John McGinlay was the man of the hour, scoring the only goal which severely dented Sweden's ambition – their second defeat in four games – and kept Scotland on the tail of Austria. A 0-0 draw with Estonia in the replay of the abandoned match was less than Brown would have wanted, but when the two sides met again a month later in March 1997 at Ibrox, the record was put straight a 2-0 victory and followed a few days later by a crucial 2-0 win over Austria at Celtic Park.

The hero of the night was the Blackburn Rovers player Kevin Gallacher – in fact he was to be the striking hero of the campaign, more than filling the boots left empty by Ferguson. Scotland had their World Cup campaign well and truly on course, but typically, just when the hard work was done, the harder work arrived.

The trip to Gothenburg to face Sweden was always going to be testing – in fact it proved too much of a test as Scotland, for the only time in the qualifying campaign, lost 2-1. This threw the group wide open and there was no change as all three of the leaders won in June 1997 – Sweden 3-2 victors in Estonia; Austria 3-1 winners in Latvia; and Scotland, thanks to a Gary McAllister penalty, victorious over Belarus in Minsk.

Two matches remained for Scotland, but it was the outcome of Sweden's visit to Austria in September 1997 that would shape their destiny. On that same evening, Scotland thumped Belarus 4-1 while Austria were 1-0 winners in Vienna.

If Scotland's nerve held, there was nothing that Sweden, now lagging behind, could do to automatically qualify, despite a 1-0 win over Latvia. Judgment day was 11 October 1997. Austria strolled home with a 4-1 victory over Belarus, but more crucial was Scotland's 2-0 win over Latvia.

Gallacher, seven goals in six matches, settled the nerves and Gordon Durie wrapped it all up with the second. This win meant Sweden's 1-0 success over Estonia was just a statistic.

As for Scotland, Gallacher had blossomed as a striker of real international quality, while Jim Leighton – at 39 years old – had enjoyed a remarkable new lease of life in goal. The proof of his effectiveness is in the figures – Scotland conceded just three goals in ten matches and scored 15. Defenders win matches and a good goalkeeper makes his defence tick.

Brown had achieved all that was expected of a Scotland side – getting to the finals – but more encouraging is the shape of the side. Not blessed with players of awe-inspiring talent, Brown has fashioned a functional team that will be desperate to remove that curse of having made seven finals and never gone past the first round.

The legends of the past – the Denis Laws and Jimmy Johnstones – are consigned to evenings of warm memories, but the likes of Gallacher, Dodds, Collins and Lambert represent one of Scotland's better chances of breaking free.

Brazil, the reigning World Champions, will present a formidable hurdle in the opening match of the tournament, but if Scotland maintains their standard of play, if they stir the fires of traditional defiance against all the odds, anything is possible. Brown will know that past Scotland sides have pulled off terrific results only to blow it against lesser lights; the prospect of Morroco and Norway after Brazil might seem like an anti-climax, but they will be anything but that – especially if Scotland are still in the tournament come the end of June.

Scottish Highlights Down the Years

There was a homely feel to the qualifying tournament for the 1954 World Cup in Switzerland. There were 38 teams wanting to be there – and Scotland found themselves duelling for the honour with England, Northern Ireland and Wales. The teams were scheduled to meet just once, in the Home International series, which doubled up as the qualifying tournament.

Scotland began with an impressive 3-1 win in Northern Ireland and followed that up with a 3-3 draw with Wales before losing 4-2 at home to England. That record of one won, one drawn and one lost was good enough to give them second place.

Expectations were high, but Scottish hopes were dented in the finals when they lost 1-0 to Austria in Zurich. Still, there have been teams who have expected far more than that who have fallen more heavily.

The second match, however, was to cruelly expose Scotland's limitations. Drawn to face Uruguay – the defending champions – Scotland were still in the game at half-time, even though they trailed 2-0. The second half was a disaster. Borges completed a hat-trick for Uruguay and Scotland were crushed 7-0. The precedent for non-progress in the finals had been set.

It was backs to the wall in 1978 for the World Cup in Argentina when everything that could go wrong did.

Qualifying ahead of Czechoslovakia and Wales, Scotland arrived in South America full of hope amid a frenzy of expectation. The Scots were the only side from the British Isles to reach the finals and, managed by Ally MacLeod, this team was built up as the best thing to come out of Scotland since sliced haggis.

The finals campaign started on 3 June in Cordoba and facing Scotland were Peru – hardly a world force in international football. Scotland, however, were about to make them look like world-beaters. Joe Jordan started the match brightly enough for Scotland, scoring after 14 minutes, but then the team went to pieces, surrendering the initiative and along with it the midfield. The beneficiary was Teofilo Cubillas, a veteran of the Peru team. He fashioned the

equalizer for Cueto a minute before half-time and then tucked away two goals in the second half – Peru 3 Scotland 1.

After the match Willie Johnston failed a random drugs test (only the second player this had happened to, the first being Ernest Jean-Joseph of Haiti four years earlier) and was sent home in disgrace. He was banned from international football for a year.

Worse was to follow in the next game against Iran, a side making their first-ever appearance in the finals and who had been crushed 3-0 by Holland in their opening match. It was imperative that Scotland won – and handsomely. Indeed, it seemed as if the gods were smiling on them when the Iranian defender Eskandarian collided with his own goalkeeper and the ball trickled into the net – own goal.

Not to be undone though, Iran came back, scored an equalizer and in the end Scotland were left feeling mighty relieved to have got the draw. Astonishingly, they were still in with a chance of making the next round – but to do that they were being asked to turn in a special performance.

Holland, losing finalists four years earlier and still masters of the Total Football concept, had to be beaten – and by three clear goals. The Dutch were not quite as incisive as they had been in West Germany and had made a slow start to the tournament, beating Iran but only drawing with Peru.

Against Scotland they were 1-0 up thanks to a first-half penalty scored by Rob Rensenbrink, but then Kenny Dalglish brought the scores level. In the second half Scotland had a penalty of their own, Archie Gemmill scored and they were ahead.

Gemmill then scored the goal of the tournament. Picking the ball up outside the penalty area, he dummied and dribbled past three Dutch defenders. Under pressure, he chipped Jongbloed and Scotland were 3-1 up – one short of the miracle they had required at kick-off. It wasn't to be. Holland hit back almost immediately when Johnny Rep hit a thunderbolt of a shot from 25 yards out. The final score stood at 3-2.

Scotland, however, as in 1967 when they became the first international side to beat England after their World Cup triumph, could claim that they had overturned Holland, a side that lost the 1978 Final to Argentina but might well have won it after hitting the post in the dying moments, a goal which would have brought them the ultimate prize.

A cloud hangs over Scotland's performances in international football, darkened by the comparative success of the auld enemy – England.

Seven World Cup finals reached plus two European Championships and on all nine occasions Scotland have failed to progress. Just to stoke the fires of frustration, England have also been successful in seven qualifying tournaments for the World Cup (nine finals appearances in total – including 1966 as hosts and 1970 as defending champions).

Yet for a country with a population of some five million, Scotland have more than played their part in the growth of world football. It was the Scots who introduced the concept of passing in the 1870s. Prior to this, players would receive the ball and dribble as far as they could until they were hacked down. Unsurprisingly, passing revolutionized the game and the next leap forward was the introduction of playing systems – the orthodox 2-3-5. Scottish club sides were also some of the first to play foreign teams but success meant that Scottish players were lured south of the border.

One of the great teams was the Scotland side of 1928 which went to Wembley and thrashed England 5-1. The Wembley Wizards, as they were known, were a class apart and the team contained the likes of Hugie Gallacher (at Newcastle), Alex James (Preston and Arsenal) and Alec Jackson (Huddersfield). The problem, however, was that these clubs were reluctant to release the players while the Scottish FA were also half pursuing a policy of not selecting Anglo-Scots.

It was not until 1950 that the World Cup called and the Home International Championship was the traditional qualifying tournament. Scotland finished behind England but then withdrew from the tournament in Brazil because they did not feel they merited a place as runners-up. The same happened in 1954, but this time there was no late retreat.

The most cherished moment, however, came on 15 April 1967 at Wembley Stadium. England, the World Champions, had played three matches since their triumph and had remained unbeaten. If ever a red rag was waved at the Scots, this was it.

England fielded the World Cup Final team bar Roger Hunt who was replaced by Jimmy Greaves. But this was to be Jim Baxter's afternoon. He taunted the England players with his ball-control and his team-mates picked up on his lead. Denis Law, Billy Bremner and Tommy Gemmell were outstanding.

Goals from Law, Bobby Lennox and Jim McCalliog earned Scotland a famous 3-2 win and a claim they they were now 'world champions'. As Bobby Charlton said after the defeat: 'If anybody had asked me who, out of all the teams in the world, will come to Wembley and beat you, I would have said the Scots. It meant more for the Scots to beat the English than it did for the English to beat the Scots.'

And in the eternal quest to put one over the English, Scotland had more cause to celebrate in 1967 when Celtic became the first British club to win the European Cup.

Scotland teams were picked by an international selection committee until 1954 when Andy Beattie was the manager – since when there have been 13 managers of the national side:

Andy Beattie	February–June 1954
Matt Busby	January–December 1958
Andy Beattie	March 1959–October 1960
Ian McColl	November 1960–May 1965
Jock Stein	June–December 1965
John Prentice	March–October 1966
Malcolm McDonald	October–November 1966
Bobby Brown	February 1967–June 1971
Tommy Docherty	October 1971–December 1972
Willie Ormond	January 1973–April 1977
Ally MacLeod	May 1977–October 1978
Jock Stein	October 1978–September 1985
Alex Ferguson	September 1985–June 1986
Andy Roxburgh	July 1986–September 1993
Craig Brown	September 1993–present

The greatest legend of Scottish football is Jock Stein. A success as a player with Celtic, he was forced to retire from the game in 1956 because of an ankle injury, and there followed a successful managerial apprenticeship, first with Dunfermline, then Hibs and finally at Celtic again.

Stein's Celtic were the side of the British Isles in the late 1960s. They dominated Scottish football and won the European Cup in 1967. Ten League titles – including nine in a row, a record matched by Rangers in 1997 – numerous domestic cups and another European final in 1970, singled them out as the side of the era. Much of their success was down to Stein, a man who transcended the religious divide of Glasgow by being a successful Protestant at Catholic Celtic.

After the Big Man was seriously injured in a car accident the general assumption was that when he recovered he would be offered a place on the Celtic board. This would have made him the club's first Protestant director – but it was not to happen. Instead, he was offered a job in the commercial department, saw this as an insult and in 1978 left to manage Leeds United – until he was summoned to Scotland's cause again.

The mark Stein made on the job of national team manager was his legacy to Scottish football. Here was the man who defined the new language of football and the term 'track-suited manager'. He got in amongst his players, drew the best out of them and had no time for prima donnas. It was claimed Stein would slap himself round the face several times before entering the changing room to give a half-time pep-talk so that it looked as though he was red with rage. Another trick he used at Celtic following a bad result on the Saturday was the Sunday morning press conference. He would tell the papers he was considering buying a new

player and this would become the Monday morning news story rather than the club's playing failures of the Saturday.

After the unmitigated disaster of the 1978 World Cup, the Scottish Football Association needed to carry out a swift and solid reconstruction job on the national team, with Stein as the top architect. Drawn in a qualifying group for 1982 with Northern Ireland, Sweden, Portugal and Israel, Scotland started their campaign with a 1-0 win in Sweden and hardly looked back from that point.

Sweden were beaten again and Israel defeated twice so that by the last qualifying match – against Portugal – a place in Spain was assured. The Portugal match in Lisbon turned out to be the only one the Scots lost, going down 2-1.

The draw in Spain was not so kind. Scotland were up against the USSR, Brazil and New Zealand. The opening game against New Zealand was fruitful enough as the Kiwis were sent packing 5-2, but Brazil proved too good. They ran out winners 4-1 and, although a 2-2 draw followed against the USSR, Scotland were out on goal difference. Stein however, had restored national pride.

Mexico 1986 was his next target, and in a tense qualifying group that had Spain at the top of the table and Iceland floundering at the bottom, the duel for the second spot was between Scotland and Wales. The decisive showdown – Ninian Park, 10 September 1985. Both teams had six points but the Scots were ahead on goal difference. Against this though, they were the away team and they were playing the game having lost the home tie 1-0. Stein inspired his side to dig deep and the match ended 1-1. But instead of jubilation, Scotland were to be knocked back as Stein suffered a massive heart-attack in the tunnel leading to the changing rooms. His players sat around gloomily waiting for more news.

'There was near silence,' says Roy Aitken, a Stein player at Celtic and with Scotland. 'We changed and waited for more news. It must have been 20 minutes later. I looked at physio Jim Steel's face and knew without any words that the worst had happened.'

Stein was dead, and so was a bit of the soul of Scottish football. Some 10,000 people lined the streets for his funeral. Scottish football would not be the same without him, even though Alex Ferguson was there to step in as a short-term caretaker of the national side.

he curse of goal-difference has derailed the progress of Scotland's World Cup finals train on more than one occasion, but hindsight means that they can look back on the 1974 finals in West Germany and pose, for that time, a unique question.

Which was the only side to play in that tournament and not lose a match?

It certainly wasn't champions West Germany. They fell 1-0 to East Germany in the first round. Holland lost their only match in the Final. That leaves Scotland with the extraordinary record of three group games played, one won and two drawn. The opposition: Brazil, Yugoslavia and Zaire.

Scotland opened against Zaire and won 2-0 with goals from Peter Lorimer and Joe Jordan, but in the final count there were not enough. Yugoslavia were to hammer the Africans 9-0 and Brazil beat them 3-0.

Even so, Scotland went into the Brazil game with everything to play for and were not overawed by the reigning World Champions. It was the fourth meeting between the two countries, the first in the World Cup, with one draw and two wins to the Brazilians. With a little bit of luck Scotland might well have won as Billy Bremner, an inspirational leader, went close, as did Lorimer and Jordan. But it was not to be and the game ended 0-0.

Scotland still had one more chance – beat Yugoslavia. A goal to Yugoslavia late on made it a difficult task, but Jordan levelled the match. However, Brazil were beating Zaire 3-0 and in the end Scotland were eliminated by one goal.

Scotland have since played Brazil on four more occasions and lost each match, while three other nations have been eliminated from the World Cup finals without losing a game – Brazil in 1978, and England and Cameroon in 1982.

s joint top scorers for their country, Kenny Dalglish and Denis Law are the kings of Scotland. They top the table with 30 goals each, but if a casting vote was needed, Law would get the nod because his 30 goals came in just 55 internationals against the 102 played by Dalglish.

Dalglish joined Celtic in 1970 and helped them to four Scottish League titles, four Scottish Cups and a Scottish League Cup, scoring 100 goals in the process before Liverpool paid a then-record fee of £440,000 for him in 1977.

South of the border he enjoyed even more success as Liverpool dominated the European Cup, winning it in 1978, 1981 and 1984, as well as collecting six League titles as a player at Anfield. He achieved the League and FA Cup double in 1986 in his first season as player-manager. He became the only man to score 100 goals both sides of the border, hitting 118 for Liverpool.

It was not always easy in the navy blue of Scotland – there was a time when the Hampden crowd jeered him and claimed that he did not play as well for his country as he did for his club sides. But Dalglish has never been one to give in and he battled through.

Fittingly, his 30th goal scored for Scotland was a cracker coming in his 96th international – a World Cup qualifier against Spain in 1984. Mo Johnston had put Scotland 2-0 ahead but then the Spanish came back with a goal. Suddenly Scotland were edgy, but Dalglish calmed the nerves when he picked up Davie Cooper's throw-in and fired home a blistering shot.

'All though my career I regarded every goal as my first or last,' said Dalglish. 'Just as long as we won, it didn't really matter.'

Dalglish went on to win another six caps without adding to his goal tally, and lives large in the memory, not just for Scotland supporters but for followers of the game throughout the world.

Denis Law was the role model for a generation of strikers and the hero of many a schoolboy – among them Kenny Dalglish. His example would not go amiss today.

'When I was younger I used to go and watch Scotland quite a bit,' said Dalglish. 'At that time most of the kids would have Denis as their favourite player and I was no different. He was really flamboyant and it was exciting to watch him, and the goals made it more spectacular and special for us kids.'

Law was born in Aberdeen and moulded as a player at Huddersfield, where he signed professional terms under Bill Shankly in 1957. By the following year Law, then 18, was winning the first of his Scotland caps. In fact at the age of 18 and 235 days he was – and still is – Scotland's youngest full international.

In 1960 he moved to Manchester City and then became one of the wave of British exports to Italian football, with a transfer to Torino. When that didn't work out however he returned to Manchester – this time United.

It was another of those golden United eras – Championships in 1965 and 1967, the FA Cup in 1963, and Law scored five hat-tricks for United in European Cup competitions. He was also voted European Footballer of the Year in 1964.

Law was a natural goal-poacher. He scored six goals in an FA Cup match for Manchester City – only to find they didn't count because the game was abandoned. In his second spell at City he scored the goal that relegated Manchester United at the end of the 1974 season when City beat United at Old Trafford. Law, however, hardly acknowledged his effort in a match that saw the wheel come full circle, because as a United player Law had scored the goal which had relegated City some ten years earlier.

With Scotland Law's haul of 55 caps was a record, his goal-scoring ratio of 0.54 per match an invaluable commodity in international football where goals are enormously hard to come by. His strengths were his shooting abilities, his speed in the penalty box and, incredibly for a man only 5'9", his heading talents – Law could soar then hover above many a giant defence.

Perhaps the pick of such headed goals came in the 1966 defeat at Hampden Park by England. Scotland lost 4-3 that day but Law's goal was a gem. Willie Johnston struck a corner, aimed at the near post, Law timed his run to perfection, rose high, arched back the trunk and literally banged the ball in with his head. Gordon Banks had no chance – and that's saying something.

Law has built up a career as a radio and TV commentator and is still admired and respected by anyone with even a passing interest in the game. It is the way he treats his peers that is admirable – not for him the belief that the past is a better place.

When Sir Matt Busby died, Law was one of the first to pay a heart-felt tribute. 'The man was totally unique,' said Law. 'He built a beautiful team in the late 1940s. He constructed the Busby Babes of the 1950s, probably his greatest team of all, so cruelly destroyed at Munich. And he came back off his death bed to produce the European Cup-winning side of 1968, just 10 years after the Munich disaster.

'But not only did he produce winning teams, he created teams full of flair and panache. He refused to play cloggers.'

Law was certainly a player of flair and panache, a man to make you think that today they don't produce them like that anymore.

 He might have won just five caps and scored a single goal – but for Jim McCalliog it was some goal; for Scotland it was a goal that made them the greatest team in the World. It was the goal that beat World Champions England at Wembley in 1967. Since then, and including that match, the two countries have met 25 times – Scotland have won five, England 15, and five have been drawn.

It is no wonder that McCalliog, a £37,500 buy for Sheffield Wednesday from Chelsea in 1965, still relishes the moment. McCalliog went on to play for and captain Wolves, turn out for Manchester United and win an FA Cup winner's medal with Southampton. But that Wembley afternoon was his first cap and McCalliog, who went into the pub business in Yorkshire after a spell at Halifax and work on PFA football in the community schemes, can still see it all clearly.

'It has to be my greatest memory,' he said. 'Winning your first cap is memorable enough and then we were playing the greatest nation in the world at that time, that made it special. So to be a part of the team that beat them was unforgettable and to get the winning goal, something else again.'

So great is the day, that the anniversary of the match is remembered – and the 25th anniversary turned into a party with McCalliog, Denis Law, Billy Bremner and Bobby Lennox there for Scotland while Bobby Moore and Nobby Stiles turned up for England.

 The quest to make it past the first round in a World Cup finals depends on Scotland coming at least second in Group A in France – made up of Brazil, Morocco and Norway.

THE RECORD TO DATE v BRAZIL

Played	8	1966 Glasgow, drew 1-1
Won	0	1972 Rio de Janeiro, lost 1-0
Lost	6	1973 Glasgow, lost 1-0
Drawn	2	1974 Frankfurt (World Cup), drew 0-0
For	2	1977 Rio de Janeiro, lost 2-0
Against	12	1990 Seville (World Cup), lost 4-1
		1987 Glasgow, lost 2-0
		1990 Turin (World Cup) lost 1-0

THE RECORD TO DATE v NORWAY

Played	11	1929 Bergen, won 7-3
Won	7	1954 Glasgow, won 1-0
Lost	1	1954 Olso, drew 1-1
Drawn	3	1963 Bergen, lost 4-3
For	30	1963 Glasgow, won 6-1
Against	14	1974 Oslo, won 2-1
		1978 Glasgow (European Championship), won 3-2
		1979 Oslo (European Championship), won 4-0
		1988 Oslo (World Cup), won 2-1
		1989 Glasgow (World Cup), drew 1-1
		1992 Oslo, drew 0-0

THE RECORD TO DATE v MOROCCO

Scotland have never played a full international against the North African country.

 Even in an otherwise empty stadium with no opposition, the Tartan Army – Scotland's fabled supporters – were there forming some sort of guard of honour. The place: Tallinn for a World Cup qualifier against Estonia – who had failed to show up. The match lasted approximately three seconds as Scotland kicked-off, then that was it.

Yet wherever they go, no matter how wild the terrain, the Tartan Army will be there to back Scotland. A shortage of tickets will be the smallest of obstacles to a nation devoted to football.

The 1970s may have seen the image of the Tartan Army tarnished by violence, but the age of video cameras and security intelligence has curbed the worst excesses – if not the fervour. Tales of men selling their houses and divorcing their wives to watch Scotland are not urban myths, many are true.

When Scotland played in the World Cup in Argentina in 1978, there was a very strong Scottish presence, and many of the supporters had hitch-hiked thousands of miles, leaving themselves open to a host of mishaps. But being there is what matters and France will be no different.

Scotland, along with England, boast the oldest international sides in the world. The first game between the two was in 1872 and ended in a 0-0 draw. In 1873 the Scottish Football Association was formed just weeks after the English FA had been founded.

International fixtures between the two countries became a regular event and between 1874 and 1887, Scotland lost just one match to England, beaten 5-4 at The Oval. That score was reversed in Glasgow the following year.

Down the years the two countries have met 108 times, England have won 44, Scotland 40 and 24 have been drawn. England have scored 190 goals to 168 for Scotland.

The Greatest Show on Earth

THERE CAN BE NO GREATER footballing high, no greater footballing low. The game is over, the World Cup has been lost and won. The trophy, bedecked in the coloured ribbons of the winning nation, glints before the eye, while all around a wall of noise invades the head. The moment has come, the winning captain steps forward, exhausted but running on the adrenaline of the moment, the hand trembles. A handshake and the trophy is handed over, lifted in triumph as the stadium noise builds even higher. It is the sort of moment you want to last forever.

For the losers the drama is witnessed in stunned disbelief, the cheers and shouts of the crowd a dull, buzzing irritant, a tinnitus hum like a painful hangover. The mind plays all sorts of tricks, posing question after question: 'Why isn't it us?' ... 'What if that shot had gone in instead of hitting the post?' ...

'Have I let my country down?'

The exhaustion is complete, the legs want to buckle but the rites of passage must be completed before the sanctuary of the dressing room and the door can be slammed shut on the chaos brought about by defeat. For the losing captain the weight of the world on the shoulders is crushing. In such moments perspectives become blurred. Reaching a World Cup Final is a mighty achievement, a source of pride. A golden moment.

So rare an honour is winning a World Cup that only six countries and 15 men have stepped forward to accept that famous trophy. It is perhaps the ultimate football list, some captains' table: Jose Nasazzi of Uruguay was the first; Combi of Italy in 1934; Meazza also of Italy in 1938; Varela when Uruguay beat Brazil in Rio de Janeiro in 1950; Walter of West Germany in 1954; Bellini of Brazil in Sweden in 1958; Gylmar the

Brazilian goalkeeper in 1962; Bobby Moore at Wembley for England in 1966; Carlos Alberto, the immaculate Brazilian defender who stood solid in Mexico in 1970. Next it was the turn of the German midfield general, Franz Beckenbauer. In 1978 another defender, Passarella of Argentina, took his turn; Dino Zoff in 1982 for Italy; Maradona was the Argentine captain in 1986; Lothar Matthaus collected it for Germany in Italy in 1990; while Dunga of Brazil was the last man to receive the prize, in the USA in 1994.

That roll call includes three goalkeepers, but astonishingly only once has a World Cup captain scored in the Final. How ironic too that it should be a defender. The man – Carlos Alberto of Brazil. The place and year – Mexico 1970. It was certainly a special World Cup, with the quality of football sublime, the matches throughout filled with drama. There was the classic England v Brazil group game, the epic West Germany against England quarter-final. Then in extra-time in their quarter-final, Italy exploded into life against Mexico, coming through to win 4-1.

In the semi-finals the Italians were involved in another extra-time thriller when beating Germany 4-3 in a ding-dong battle. Then the Final, the artistry of Brazil being given a full canvas as they won 4-1. As for Carlos Alberto's goal – it was worth the wait. Brazil

were 3-1 ahead and four minutes remained. Jairzinho found Pelé with a perfectly weighted through-pass; he controlled it as only Pelé could and, aware of everything that was happening around him, laid the ball off for his captain to crash home a powerful shot.

No captain, as the list proves, has ever lifted the trophy twice although Maradona was skipper of Argentina when they won in 1986 and lost in 1990, while the German Karl-Heinz Rummenigge was twice the skipper of losing finalists.

AT THE START of the World Cup in 1930 only two of the 13 teams who took part were founder members of FIFA – France and Belgium. By the 1994 World Cup in America 144 teams dreamed of playing in the finals of the World Cup and 24 made it. For France '98 the number has grown again – and so too have the finalists. There will be 32 countries playing before the biggest TV audience ever, and a live crowd that has swelled dramatically tournament on tournament.

The number of spectators in Chile in 1962 was 896,336. The figure had climbed to 2,517,348 in Italia '90 and then 3,587,538 in the USA. The expanded format of the finals in France will see live attendances shoot up again.

Little Acorns – Mighty Oaks

IN THE BEGINNING there were 13 invited teams – some grateful guests, others cajoled and threatened – but there were enough to make a competition of it and Uruguay, the hosts celebrating the 100th year of their independence, won.

Now, 68 years on for France '98, the 13 have grown to a staggering 172 all wanting to be there. They have to be whittled down by the five world-wide federations to a manageable 32 – and even that figure is the most yet for the finals stage of the World Cup.

Every World Cup cycle has seen the number of nations wanting to compete grow – with one exception – and 1978 was the watershed year when the number taking part broke the three-figure barrier as 106 nations tried to reach Argentina. There folllowed 109 for Spain in 1982, 121 for Mexico in 1986, 112 for Italy in 1990 then 144 in the USA in 1994.

As the numbers of the wannabes climb higher, so the figures for the 'been there, done it' brigade stay constant. There have been only six winners over the years and all of them – bar England – have carried away the trophy more than once. Only ten nations, in various permutations, have contested the Final.

Down the years the World Cup has reflected the changing world, nations have come and gone, great powers like the USSR have fractured and become multiple countries; Ukraine, Belarus, Estonia, Latvia, Georgia, to name but a few of the pieces left by the fallout. New awareness and new territories have created other challengers. China now has real pretensions when it comes to the World Cup and although they failed to qualify this time, there is no doubt they'll be back.

The biggest expectations, however, are for one of the African nations. When Cameroon made the 1982 finals in Spain they were just another exotic outsider, there to make up the numbers. Eight years later they were back – proving to be far more than just day-trippers. They beat the World Cup holders Argentina 1-0 in the tournament's opening game and then just went on and on.

In the group stages they beat Romania 2-1 and were through to the last 16. On they marched, scoring a thrilling extra-time win over Colombia for a quarter-final spot against England. England, the country that gave football to the world, needed extra-time to see off the challenge of the vibrant and colourful Africans.

Even then victory came courtesy of a huge helping of luck. England went ahead, Cameroon levelled the match and then took the lead. Time was running out and England were looking to be in desperate trouble when Gary Lineker burst into the Cameroon penalty area and was fouled. He got up to score from the spot and was to do exactly the same in extra-time. But Cameroon might well have sprung a major shock.

And that is the beauty of the World Cup – surprises are always possible. Back in 1966, the men from North Korea knocked Italy out thanks to a 1-0 group win and then were 3-0 up against Portugal in the quarter-final before being beaten 5-3. Magic, romance and eye-rubbing 'I can't believe it' stuff.

And so to France. Africa is the quarter from which the surprises are expected. Cameroon may be a little past their sell-by date, but the real threat could be posed by Nigeria – the Olympic football champions. The World Cup is littered with great sides that have evolved from Olympic teams – like the Hungary of the Mighty Magyars in the 1950s, unbeaten between 1951 and 1956 except for the World Cup Final of 1954, when they lost 3-2 to West Germany in Berne.

Then the established teams will take some shifting. South American sides might have a reputation for not doing too well in World Cups in Europe, but few can expect a Brazilian side that includes Romário and Ronaldo to fold that easily. Brazil are the proud holders of the cup, the only side to have won it four times and they are desperate to win it again.

Germany – once successful West Germany and less successful East Germany – another nation changed by political history and unified, are almost certain to pose a threat. Even when the side is not glittering with talent, it has a frighteningly functional approach that has been a proven winner time and again. Germany are the current European Champions and will be hard to beat.

Holland have the players of flair and style, as well as the tendency to have a tantrum. If all is well they will be a dangerous side, as will the Italians who were forced into the ignominy of a play-off game against Russia to make it in the first place.

A host nation has not won the World Cup for 20 years – when Argentina beat Holland 3-1 in Buenos Aires – but then Spain, Mexico and the USA, three of the next four host countries, do not have the greatest of World Cup traditions even if they have sparkled on occasions.

This time France look a strong side. They won their only major international trophy at home in the European Championship of 1984, when Michel Platini led France to beat Spain in the Final, and that will be seen as an omen. Their players are scattered around Europe, playing for the best teams in Italy, Spain and England, and they have the flair to do well.

England, too, are a side coming into form. Young and benefitting from the influx of top overseas players into the Premier League, which in turn has raised the standard, their ambitions are built upon real foundations.

As the number of contestants to the finals has grown, so too has the coverage, the spin-offs from the competition, the merchandise. More matches than ever in France will in turn lead to the highest ever number of spectators attending live games – and the television viewing figures will be astronomical. From the middle of the hottest desert to the heart of the coldest ice cap, televisions will be tuned to the greatest show on earth – it is some claim to make, but as the past has proved and the future leads us to expect, the World Cup is just that.

The Growth of the World Cup

1930

THE IDEA WAS BRILLIANT – but selling it was a completely different matter. It started with just 13 teams and came about after plenty of wheeling and dealing in the corridors outside committee rooms and many hours of heated discussions and angry exchanges within. Yet to have got 13 teams, an agreed host nation and the organization in place was a minor miracle considering the strangulated gestation of the idea. Today the World Cup is the single greatest sporting event – growing with every turn of its four-year cycle.

The brainchild of two Frenchmen, Jules Rimet and Henri Delaunay, the idea was conceived in 1904 at the first meeting of FIFA, but it was to be another 16 years (at the Olympic Games in Antwerp in 1920) before the movement began to gain momentum.

One of the major problems was that the British football associations – the ones responsible for giving the world the game of football and then introducing a formalized structure for it – were suspicious of the whole FIFA concept. Here was a global body formed by seven European nations, three of them without their own national football associations. On top of that, France had only played their first international 20 days before the meeting, something that three other countries at the meeting – Spain, Denmark and Switzerland – were yet to do.

Not wishing to seem churlish, the British joined – but then withdrew in 1928, angry at the way the demarcation lines between amateur and professional were being blurred. This was a problem the British

had settled back in 1883, but in Europe and South America 'broken time' payments (money paid to players for time off work) were either openly allowed or paid discreetly, allowing the players concerned to keep their amateur status. British objections at this point centred around the Olympic Games football tournament – the only world championship of any kind and one which the British felt should adhere strictly to the amateur ethos.

And so, on 26 May 1928, the first World Cup started to take shape without England, Wales, Scotland and Ireland. FIFA, presided over by Rimet, announced the competition and offered an open invite to the footballing nations of the world.

Next, a host country had to be found. FIFA met on 18 May 1929 to consider the claims of Italy, Holland, Spain, Sweden and Uruguay. It was the South American country which made the most passionate pitch – 1930 was the centenary of their independence and they pledged to build a new stadium for the competition. Perhaps the most persuasive argument of all, however, was the promise to foot the bill for the other participating nations.

Uruguay got the nod, whereupon Austria, Czechoslovakia, Germany and Switzerland said they were not going – South America was too far away (three weeks by boat). Tit for tat, the South American nations threatened to quit FIFA because of the snub and another compromise had to be thrashed out.

Belgium, France, Romania and Yugoslavia were persuaded to go and take up the challenge of Argentina, Bolivia, Brazil, Chile, Mexico, Paraguay, the USA (then made up of former English and Scottish professionals), Peru and of course the host nation.

The Belgians, French and Romanians set sail on the *Conte Verde* on 21 June 1930 and on the Sunday afternoon of 13 July 1930 France and Mexico played the first-ever World Cup match. There was controversy when, ten minutes into the game, the French goalkeeper Alex Thépot took a kick in the jaw and had to leave the field. This was in the days before substitutes, but even so the French triumphed 4-1. Yet they failed to make the semi-finals after another controversial match – a 1-0 defeat by Argentina in a game that ended six minutes early when the referee blew up for full-time just as France seemed poised to equalize. In a

contest structured so that it pitched together the winners from the four groups, Argentina, Yugoslavia, the USA and Uruguay remained.

The USA had not conceded a goal in the tournament, but were swept away 6-1 by Argentina and the other semi-final showed an equally high score as Yugoslavia were trounced 6-1 by Uruguay.

And so to the Centenario Stadium in Montevideo, filled to its 100,000 capacity for Uruguay against Argentina – to be played on 17 July, Uruguay's Independence day. These two countries were bitter rivals and an endless procession of boats had crossed the River Plate from Buenos Aires to Montevideo, the Argentines chanting 'Victory or Death'.

The match was 12 minutes old when Pablo Dorado put Uruguay ahead; but then Peucelle equalized and in the 37th minute, Stábile, the tournament's leading scorer with eight goals, made it 2-1 to Argentina with a goal the home crowd claimed was offside. At half-time the home fans wept and prayed. And those prayers were answered. Pedro Cea made it 2-2, then in the 68th minute Santos Iriarte put Uruguay ahead, leaving Castro to score the fourth in the closing seconds.

Jose Nasazzi stepped forward to collect the 30cm gold trophy, the 'Victoire aux auiles d'or' – sculpted by Frenchman Abel Lafleur – as Montevideo went mad. In Argentina, the Uruguayan embassy was stoned and the crowd cleared away only after the police opened fire. The World Cup had arrived.

1954

THE SECOND WORLD WAR had come and gone and the World Cup had been contested three more times since Uruguay triumphed in the first tournament – won by Italy in 1934, successfully defended by them in 1938 and then claimed again by Uruguay in 1950.

By the time the competition headed for Switzerland in 1954, there were 38 nations wanting to play in the tournament and this number had been whittled down to 16 – split into four groups of four. One of the problems had been the exact format of the finals, up to this point a strange mish-mash of straight knock-out matches and a league system with no designated Final. In Switzerland it was going to be straightforward, but even then a spanner was thrown into the works of simplicity.

There would be two seeded teams in each group and they would not face each other. That meant that each side played two group games and the weakest faced the strongest. Such a system was open to cynical calculation by the teams, as Germany in Group Two proved. The team they wanted to avoid was Brazil so they worked out that by losing to Hungary – they sent out a virtual reserve team and were beaten 8-3 – they then had to beat Turkey in a play-off match. They did so, winning 7-2 to earn a quarter-final match against Yugoslavia.

Yet the intricacies of the system should not cloud the beauty of the game and this special era. This was the age of the superb Hungarian side – the Mighty Magyars as the British press had dubbed them, a description that was unerring in its accuracy. This was the Hungary of Ferenc Puskás, Nandor Hidegkuti, Josef Bozsik, Sandor Kocsis and Zoltan Czibor. They were to lose only one match between 1950 and 1956 and could boast 6-3 and 7-1 wins over England. The tragedy was in the timing of that one defeat – but more of that later.

England, seeded in Group Four, drew 4-4 with Belgium and beat Switzerland 2-0 to earn a quarter-

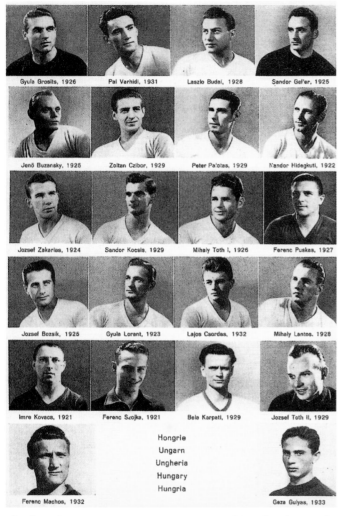

Gyula Grosits, 1926   Pal Varhidi, 1931   Laszlo Budai, 1928   Sandor Gel'er, 1925

Jenö Buzansky, 1925   Zoltan Czibor, 1929   Peter Pa'otas, 1929   N'andor Hidegkuti, 1922

Jozsef Zakarias, 1924   Sandor Kocsis, 1929   Mihaly Toth I, 1926   Ferenc Puskas, 1927

Jozsef Bozsik, 1925   Gyula Lorant, 1923   Lajos Csordas, 1932   Mihaly Lantos, 1928

Imre Kovacs, 1921   Ferenc Szojka, 1921   Bela Karpati, 1929   Jozsef Toth II, 1929

Hongrie
Ungarn
Ungheria
Hungary
Hungria

Ferenc Machos, 1932   Geza Gulyas, 1933

final with Uruguay, 7-0 conquerors of Scotland. Brazil reached the last eight, as did Switzerland via a play-off with Italy. Yet Hungary, who had faced Germany in a group match, had suffered a severe blow when Puskás had been deliberately kicked on the ankle by Werner Liebrich, the West German centre-half, and was left on the sidelines until the Final.

The Germans cantered through to the semi-finals after a 2-0 quarter-final win over Yugoslavia, but Hungary had the tough one – against Brazil. On paper it should have been a match of footballing magic, but the reality was very different as the two sides became embroiled in an infamous match known as 'The Battle of Berne'.

Hungary, in typical swirling, dazzling style, were 2-0 up in seven minutes, but a series of niggling fouls by the Hungarians lit a fuse. Two penalties, the first to Brazil and the second to Hungary in the 61st minute made it 3-1 but only succeeded in fanning the flames. Brazil clawed back to 3-2, then Bozsik and Nilton Santos of Brazil were at each other. The referee sent them off as already vicious tackles became down-right nasty. Hungary scored a fourth and won 4-2 but then the two sides became involved in a dressing-room brawl.

Meanwhile Austria won a finals epic, conquering Switzerland 7-5 in a match that had five goals in one ten-minute period, while Uruguay – yet to lose a match in the World Cup finals – came through 4-2 against England. The semi-finals were Germany against Austria and Hungary against Uruguay.

The muscular Germans powered past a technically superior Austria with a resounding 6-1 win while Hungary and Uruguay were involved in a titanic battle that still stands as one of the great games in World Cup history. Hungary were 2-0 up, but Uruguay would not give up and Juan Eduardo Hohberg levelled the scores. Extra-time was played and Uruguay, visibly tiring, were beaten 4-2. 'We beat the best team we ever met,' said Gyula Mandi, the Hungarian manager, graciously.

And so to the Final in Berne with Hungary the out-and-out favourites. Puskás came back, but the power of hindsight shows it to be the wrong decision. True to form Hungary were 2-0 up after eight minutes, Puskás scoring one of the goals, Czibor the other, yet the Germans would not roll over.

Inspired by the sensational goalkeeping of Toni Turek and the drive of Helmut Rahn, the Germans pulled back to 2-2 by half-time. Hungary, with Puskás struggling, were clearly unbalanced and the Germans could sense it. Five minutes remained when Rahn found himself with four defenders ahead of him; he made space and delivered the perfect shot. It was 3-2 to Germany.

Time was running out, but Hungary kept going. Puskás had the ball in the net but the goal was controversially disallowed for offside. Germany hung on for a 3-2 win and Hungary had lost one fateful match in an otherwise incredible six-year undefeated run.

They had earned the unwanted albatross of praise – the greatest team never to have won the World Cup.

1966

N EURO '96 THE ENGLAND FANS sang about football coming home. It had, but not quite in the same way as it did in 1966 – a date of more historical significance to England football fans than 1066 and all that.

This was the year England hosted the tournament and it was the year they became only the fifth country to win the World Cup, making the most of home advantage. It had been decided that whoever won the Jules Rimet trophy for a third time would keep it forever and in 1966 Italy, Uruguay and Brazil entered the competition with a chance of taking that honour.

Bigger and better than ever, there were 71 teams vying for a place in the finals, the holders Brazil and hosts England finally joined by 14 other sides, whittled down through the qualifying tournament. This brought the likes of North Korea and Portugal to the contest, and both these sides were to light up the show with some superb performances.

England opened with a 0-0 draw against Uruguay, but it was the 5-0 victory for West Germany over Switzerland in Group Two which rang the loudest warning bells. The shock was the demise of the defending champions Brazil.

They opened with a comfortable enough win over Bulgaria, scoring twice and conceding none, but in the course of the game Pelé was scythed down and forced to sit out the next match – against Hungary. And here it started to go wrong. Hungary won 3-1, leaving the Brazilians needing a win from their last group match with Portugal. Inspired by Eusébio – one of the stars of 1966 – Portugal won 3-1; Brazil were out of the tournament and Pelé – back in the side but again singled out for some rough treatment – returned home vowing never to play in a World Cup again.

England, meanwhile, had beaten Mexico and France 2-0 to qualify for the quarter-finals, where they were joined by Uruguay. In Group Two Germany and

Argentina went through, while Group Three provided Portugal and Hungary. The shock was in Group Four. The USSR were expected to progress but so too were the Italians.

Instead, playing North Korea at Ayresome Park – the former home of Middlesbrough – Park Doo-ik, an army dentist, scored the only goal of the game to send Italy home early. They met with a hostile reception at Genoa Airport, where they were pelted with rotten fruit – not so much 'just one cornetto' as a 'fistful of mouldy tomatoes'.

North Korea then faced Portugal in the quarter-final at Goodison Park and within 24 minutes were 3-0 up. However, they lacked experience on the international stage, did not know how to close the game down and Eusébio galvanized his side by scoring four goals in 34 minutes. In the end Eusébio – who was to finish the tournament top scorer with nine goals – had turned it around as Portugal won 5-3.

Germany thumped Uruguay 4-0 and the USSR won 2-1 against Hungary. That left England against Argentina to play out a game every bit as notorious as 'The Battle of Berne' between Brazil and Hungary in Switzerland in 1954.

It was clear that Argentina were technically a highly-skilled side, but their fatal flaw was their temperament. Poisoned by a vicious, cynical streak, the Argentine players fouled just about anything that moved, and the worst culprit was their captain Antonio Rattin. While all around him team-mates were being booked, Rattin continued to hack away, impervious to warnings from the referee.

Something had to give and it was the referee's patience. He sent Rattin off, but he refused to go and for 11 minutes the Argentine players argued the case, until eventually Rattin left. England won 1-0 but at the end Alf Ramsey ran on to the pitch to tell his players not to swap shirts with their opponents. He was to go on to call his rivals 'animals', although he later apologized for his remark.

Ramsey, appointed in 1962, was the first England manager to be given *carte blanche* with selection and his loyalty to his players was absolute. In the group match with France, Nobby Stiles had put in a crude tackle on a French player right beneath the Royal Box at Wembley where some of the FA hierarchy were sitting. They insisted that Ramsey should drop Stiles for the next match, but Ramsey was having none of it. He said he would rather resign.

Germany beat the USSR to reach the Final while two great goals from Bobby Charlton saw England past Portugal, both semi-finals ending 2-1.

It was to be a classic Final, still clouded today by controversy over England's third goal. Germany took first blood after 13 minutes; Helmut Haller pounced on Ray Wilson's poor clearance and bingo.

Geoff Hurst headed the equalizer from Bobby Moore's quick free-kick and then in the second half Hurst's West Ham colleague Peters added the second. England clung on, but in the dying moments of the game Weber scored Germany's second.

'You've beaten them once – now you've got to do it again,' said Ramsey as he geed up his men for extra-time. 'Look at them, they're finished.'

Indeed they were. Hurst, with his back to goal, swivelled and shot from Alan Ball's cross and the ball crashed against the bar then bounced down. Roger Hunt, following up, raised his arms in celebration and the referee, following confirmation from the Russian linesman Bakhramov, awarded the goal. Slow-motion film fails to prove conclusively one way or the other whether the ball had crossed the line, and even today Germans will argue that it did not.

Hurst, however, settled the issue with the last kick of the match, latching on to Moore's long clearance and blasting the ball home to become the first and to date the only man to score a hat-trick in a World Cup Final. Moore collected the trophy and England, home of the Swinging Sixties revolution, went into party mode.

1970

ENGLAND WENT TO MEXICO to defend their trophy, and they put up a brave fight – but this was a tournament to mark the return of Brazil to their brilliant best; a fitting finale for Pelé, still the world's greatest player, to strut for a final time on such a grand stage. It was also to mark the emergence of new stars.

Once again there were four groups of four teams, and in Group One the hosts Mexico finished behind the USSR to qualify for the quarter-finals. Group Two had Italy and Uruguay as qualifiers although Israel, eliminated in fourth place along with Sweden, had come away from their first finals with one defeat and two draws.

The real interest was in Group Three, where England and Brazil were together, along with Romania and Czechoslovakia. As soon as the groups became known, the clash between the defending champions and the soon-to-be crowned champions was billed as 'the real Final'. It was a match that lived up to all expectations. Alf Ramsey was still in charge and had the core of the England squad that had succeeded four years earlier, supplemented by talented newcomers such as Terry Cooper, Alan Mullery and Francis Lee. Brazil too had fresh faces: Jairzinho, Rivelino and Tostão.

Mexico in June is hot at the best of times, hotter still at noon – the scheduled time for the kick-off at the behest of the television companies. This meant temperatures of almost 100°F. On top of that, the England squad had hardly slept the previous night, kept awake by Brazilian fans who had surrounded the team's hotel to chant all night.

Yet England were worthy World Champions, mad dogs and Englishmen prepared to go out in the midday sun. The intent

to hang on to their trophy was there for all to see after ten minutes. Jairzinho burst down the wing; Gordon Banks, the England goal-keeper, moved to his near post; the cross was whipped in as Pelé came storming into the middle of the penalty area, and he climbed majestically and powered his header down towards the far post. He was wheeling away yelling as Banks crossed his goal, twisted and turned in his dive – and forced the ball away for the greatest save ever.

There was nothing Banks could do in the second half, however, when Tostão launched the killer move, racing past three defenders, playing the ball on to Pelé who found Jairzinho and it was in the net. Jairzinho, though not the top scorer in Mexico, was to notch up a goal in every match Brazil played.

England stormed back and laid siege to the Brazilian goal, squandered a number of gilt edged chances and had to face a 1-0 defeat. The consequences of which were a quarter-final with the old foe, West Germany. Brazil were to go on and beat Peru 4-2, while Uruguay won 1-0 in extra-time against the USSR and Italy needed extra-time to conquer Mexico 4-1.

Now came the England-Germany match. England suffered a blow when goalkeeper Gordon Banks had to withdraw because of food poisoning, thought to have been picked up from a bottle of beer. This meant Peter Bonetti took his place. Still, there was no panic for England. They led 1-0 at half-time thanks to an Alan Mullery goal, and were ahead 2-0

with just over 20 minutes to play after Martin Peters scored in the 50th minute.

Then – disaster. A Franz Beckenbauer shot squeezed under Bonetti's body and England started to flag. Ramsey played his substitutes' card, but changed the balance of his team and eight minutes from the end Uwe Seeler's header levelled the scores at 2-2. In extra-time there was only ever going to be one winner and it was Gerd Müller who wrapped it up, 3-2. Sweet revenge for Germany.

Already Mexico 1970 had served up a feast of football, but there was more to come in the pulsating semi-final between Italy and Germany. The Italians were following a tactic of defence as the only form of attack, being content to sneak a goal and soak up the pressure. They led 1-0 until Karl-Heinz Schnellinger scored in the third minute of injury time. Extra-time and the floodgates opened. Müller put the Germans ahead, the Italians scored twice before Müller levelled it again and finally Rivera clinched it 4-3 for Italy.

Italy were now faced with Brazil – comfortable 3-1 conquerors of Uruguay – in the Final and Pelé opened the scoring. Italy levelled, but then Brazil cut loose in the second half after Gérson scored in the 66th minute. Pelé laid the ball on for Jairzinho to sweep home the third before Carlos Alberto finished it off with a thundering shot. Brazil were worthy champions, the Jules Rimet trophy was theirs to keep and Mexico '70 had been a World Cup to savour in the memory.

1974

I F IN THE 1950s HUNGARY were saddled with the title 'the best team never to have won the World Cup', then the 1970s marked a decade when that crown was passed on – to Holland.

This was the age of Total Football, a Dutch invention that did away with players sticking to a rigid format and instead allowed them to rotate. If a defender moved into attack, an attacker would move back to defend. It was a system that required complete concentration, swift thought, but above all, men who could play football, men comfortable on the ball.

The Dutch were lucky. On that front they had a very special team – Johan Cruyff and Johan Neeskens were just two stars in a team of real players. As their coach Rinus Michels said: 'You need at least seven world-class players to use the system; one less and you are in trouble.'

At the outset there had been 98 teams bidding to make the finals in West Germany, and England had fallen by the wayside, eliminated in the qualifying stages by Poland. The East European side were to be a force in the competition, coming through their Group Four matches with three wins out of three, including victories over Italy and Argentina, and a tally of 12 goals scored against three conceded.

In Group Three Holland were frighteningly good, strolling past Uruguay 2-0, held by a battling Sweden to 0-0 and then destroying Bulgaria 4-1. Meanwhile in Group Two Scotland – the lone British representatives – were to be punished for a lack of goals against Zaire. The group boiled down to who could score the most against the African side. Scotland won 2-0, Brazil 3-0 and Yugoslavia 9-0. Yugoslavia and Brazil progressed and Scotland were in familiar territory, the airport lounge looking for an early plane home.

Group One was all about Germany, both East and West qualifying, East having the better of the game between the two countries and winning 1-0. So on to stage two.

A new round of group matches had Holland, Brazil, East Germany and Argentina in section A while section B had West Germany, Poland, Sweden and Yugoslavia. By this stage the teams were well into their stride and the Dutch were getting better and better.

Argentina were crushed 4-0, East Germany 2-0 and Brazil also 2-0. Brazil, now without Pelé and running on a tank of memories, scored one superb goal against East Germany when Rivelino struck a wickedly swerving free-kick in their 1-0 win. That apart, they were second best to the Dutch.

Group B was a much closer affair, with West Germany far from confident in beating Yugoslavia 2-0 and Sweden 4-2. This left them in a head to head with Poland who had beaten Sweden 1-0 and Yugoslavia 2-1. It was a winner-takes-all contest played on a waterlogged pitch that favoured the more muscular

Germans. There was drama along the way with Jan Tomaszewski saving a penalty, but helpless when a deflected shot ran into the path of Gerd Müller, who scored the only goal of the game. Poland went on to take third place after a play-off with Brazil, but all eyes were on the Final in Munich and what should have been the crowning moment for Dutch football.

Indeed, the way the game started it looked as though Holland would take it at a canter. The kick-off was Holland's and they played the ball forward with a series of neat passes, not a German player getting near the ball. As Cruyff strode into the penalty area, he was brought down by Hoeness. Penalty – and Neeskens scored, 1-0 to Holland, only two minutes gone and a German yet to kick the ball.

Holland's technical supremacy bordered on the arrogant, but Germany were not going to give up without a fight and were level when they won a penalty and Breitner scored. Two minutes before half-time Gerd Müller put them ahead when he controlled

a less-than-perfect cross from Bonhof, dragged the ball back and fired home a shot past Jan Jongbloed. It was Müller's 68th and final goal for his country – and the most important of the lot.

The second half belonged totally to Holland, but Sepp Maier in the German goal would not be beaten and when he foiled Neeskens with one stunning save, the Dutch seemed to realize that this was not going to be their day. In the end pragmatic football had won out but Holland had given the game a new direction.

A look at the tournament's leading goalscorers is proof that their talk of Total Football was not hot air. They scored 15 goals during the competition, of which Neeskens hit five and Johnny Rep four, the rest shared between a team of players willing to take on the responsibility themselves.

Holland were to reach the Final again in 1978 in Argentina, where they lost 3-1 to the hosts in extra-time. They were still playing Total Football, but perhaps did not quite have the required number of world-class players to carry it off convincingly. For all that it was a joy to watch and although they won nothing, they certainly brought some footballing sunshine to the 1970s.

1990

BIGGER IS NOT ALWAYS better, as Italia '90 proved. There were 112 sides bidding to make the finals – and there were 24 teams involved in those final stages. Yet such was the value of the prize that the negative rather than the positive came to the fore. This was a World Cup that suffered an acute shortage of goals – a meagre 115 in 52 games. Worse, there were 164 bookings and 16 sendings-off. The stars to illuminate the stage never made it out of the wings.

But for all that there were great moments and heartening ones. None more so than the England revival – a fabulous run that took them to the semi-final and, but for a penalty shoot-out failure, would have led to the Final and surely victory over a desperately poor Argentina.

The competition started in sensational style when Cameroon kicked-off against defending champions Argentina, ignored the script when Omam Biyik put them ahead and then had the nerve to hold on for victory. African football had arrived.

Argentina were to squeeze through to the last 16 by the skin of their teeth; Cameroon, despite a Group B 4-0 drubbing by the already eliminated

USSR, went forward more confidently. In Group A Italy, with three wins out of three and a new hero in Toto Schillaci, advanced easily enough with Czechoslovakia. Brazil had no problems in Group C but did not really appear to be firing and made heavy weather of all three matches, the last a 1-0 win over Scotland. Costa Rica were the surprise runners-up, having beaten both Scotland and Sweden. Group D belonged to Germany and Group E to Spain.

England were in Group F with Holland, the Republic of Ireland and Egypt. There were six matches played and only one positive result, England beating Egypt 1-0 while drawing 1-1 with Ireland and 0-0 with Holland.

The last 16 followed a knockout format and Cameroon kept marching on, beating Colombia 2-1 in extra-time. Czechoslovakia thumped Costa Rica 4-1 while Brazil succumbed 1-0 to Argentina. The match of the round was between West Germany and Holland. A fiery encounter, which saw Germany's Rudi Völler and Holland's Frank Rijkaard sent off after a spitting and then push-and-shove incident, was settled 2-1 in Germany's favour.

The Republic of Ireland's terrific run continued, thanks to a penalty shoot-out success over Romania, winning 5-4 after a 0-0 draw, while Italy were 2-0 winners over Uruguay. Spain lost 2-1 to Yugoslavia in extra-time and England beat Belgium with the last kick of extra-time. Penalties were looming when a free-kick was hoisted into the heart of the Belgian defence. England's David Platt swivelled and volleyed home for a goal that broke Belgian hearts.

In the quarter-finals Argentina revealed their true colours, coming through against Yugoslavia on penalties after a 0-0 draw. Ireland lost 1-0 to Italy – but were to beat them memorably by the same margin in New York four years later – while Germany were 1-0 conquerors of Czechoslavakia. England were made to battle on against Cameroon.

The African nation went behind to a David Platt goal, levelled through a penalty 16 minutes into the second half and then went ahead four minutes later. England seemed incapable of breaching the Africans' stout defence, but a trip on Gary Lineker gave England a chink of light that was looking increasingly unlikely. Extra-time, Lineker was fouled in the box again and England were through to their first World Cup semi-final on foreign soil.

Both matches were tight. Italy and Argentina drew 1-1 and went to penalties where Argentina won and a host nation sobbed. England also drew 1-1 with Germany and again it was penalties. Chris Waddle and Stuart Pearce were denied and Germany were on their way to a third World Cup triumph. Memories of what might have been, of Gascoigne's tears, of Lineker's goals, still haunt every England fan.

The Final was a drab affair ruined by Argentina's intentions to go for the draw and the lottery of the penalty shoot-out. Instead it was a penalty late in the game which settled it. Völler went down in the box, Brehme calmly converted the kick and that was it. Two Argentines were sent off and a world rejoiced that the South Americans – true pantomime villains in Italy – had not made off with football's crown jewel, the World Cup.

GROUP A

Brazil

(DEFENDING CHAMPIONS)

WORLD CUP RECORD

This is the country that sets the standards for all the others. Winners of three World Cups so that they got to keep the Jules Rimet trophy, they have since added the new trophy to the cabinet to claim four World Cup wins – more than any other nation. The names, down the years, still roll off the tongue – Pelé, Didi, Garrincha, Rivelino, Jairzinho, Zico and Socrates. The first World Cup was claimed in Sweden in 1958 where they won two of their three group matches – the blot was a 0-0 draw with England – then went on to knock out Wales 1-0 in the quarter-final. Then they really hit form, beating France 5-2 in the semi-final and hosts Sweden by the same margin in the Final. Amazingly, the Swedes went ahead but it was the magic of 17-year-old Pelé – he scored twice in the Final – that swung the contest. Four years later Brazil defended the trophy successfully – and without an injured Pelé. Spain and Mexico were beaten in the group stages then England were dispatched 3-1 in the quarter-finals. As in Sweden, Brazil saved their goalscoring spree for later in the tournament, beating hosts Chile 4-2 in the semi-final and Czechoslovakia 3-1 in the Final.

Disappointing in 1966, where they failed to progress past the group stage, Brazil were back on song in Mexico in 1970 with, Pelé apart, a side of new heroes. Jairzinho scored in every round as Brazil came through the group stage with three wins out of three;

crushed Peru 4-2 in the quarter-final; Uruguay 3-1 in the semi-final; and then demolished Italy 4-1. Pelé, putting the icing on a brilliant career, scored in the Final as Brazil made off with the cup for keeps. In 1974 they reached the second round, but a period of slump had set in. They qualified for every tournament onwards but it was not until America in 1994 that they really started to live up to their reputation. A last-16 win over the USA was followed by a thrilling quarter-final clash with Holland, Brazil winning 3-2. Sweden were beaten 1-0 in the semi-final and next up were Italy. The game, despite the stars on the field, was dire and drifted through extra-time at 0-0 with penalties to decide the issue. When Roberto Baggio missed with Italy's fifth and final penalty, Brazil were crowned World Champions. Today, with stars like Ronaldo and Bebeto, Brazil are a major and feared force.

KEY PLAYERS

ROBERTO CARLOS Age: 24 Club: Real Madrid (Spain)

◆ With over 40 caps, Roberto Carlos is a regular at international level and was an ever-present during Brazil's Copa América triumph in the summer of 1997.

◆ He is rated one of the best left-backs in the world, although he claims Paolo Maldini is still better: 'He's more experienced but I hope to overtake him soon.'

RONALDO Age: 21 Club: Inter Milan (Italy)

◆ Ronaldo is already being cited as Brazil's greatest talent since Pelé.

◆ At 16, he scored 54 goals in 54 matches in the Brazilian First Division and at 18, he scored 55 goals in 56 matches for PSV Eindhoven.

◆ Twice breaking the world record transfer fee, he moved to Barcelona and then for £18 million to Inter Milan in July 1997.

DENILSON Age: 20 Club: São Paulo

◆ Denilson is rumoured to be signing a £21.5 million deal with Spanish side Real Betis – which would make him the most expensive player in the world.

◆ A left-footed midfielder, he was a member of the Brazilian team that reached the Final of the 1995 World Youth Cup.

MANAGER | **PROFILE**

MARIO JORGE LOBO ZAGALLO

An old head, Mario Jorge Lobo Zagallo has been coaching national sides since 1970 when he was at the helm with Brazil for four years. He spent time with Kuwait, Saudi Arabia and the United Arab Emirates before picking up the reins with Brazil again in 1994. He was part of the backroom team to the 1994 winning side in the USA before moving into the hot-seat again. Zagallo, now 66, played with Rio de Janeiro sides América, Flamengo, Botafogo and won 37 caps and two World Cups.

GROUP A

Morocco

ROAD TO FRANCE

Morocco 4 Sierra Leone 0 (9 November 1996)   Sierra Leone 0 Morocco 1 (26 April 1997)
Ghana 2 Morocco 2 (12 January 1997)   Morocco 1 Ghana 0 (7 June 1997)
Gabon 0 Morocco 4 (6 April 1997)   Morocco 2 Gabon 0 (17 August 1997)

WORLD CUP RECORD

First qualified for the finals back in Mexico in 1970, but by the time they had managed a 1-1 draw with Bulgaria they were out – having lost 2-1 to Germany and 3-0 to Peru. It was to be another 16 years before Morocco were back in the finals – and once again it was Mexico. This time they fared much better in their group, drawing 0-0 with Poland, 0-0 with England and then crushing Portugal 3-1. That was good enough to take them through to the last 16 where, after putting up a terrific fight, they were beaten 1-0 by eventual finalists West Germany. There was no such happy outcome from the trip to America in 1994 when they lost all three of their group matches, beaten 1-0 by Belgium, 2-1 by Saudi Arabia and 2-1 by Holland. Regular participants in the African Nations Cup, they have one triumph – in 1976.

KEY PLAYERS

SALAHEDDINE BASSIR

Age: 25 **Club:** Deportivo La Coruna (Spain)

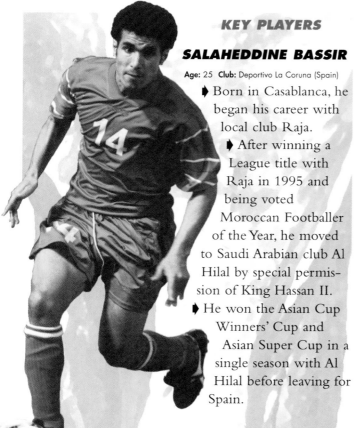

◗ Born in Casablanca, he began his career with local club Raja.
◗ After winning a League title with Raja in 1995 and being voted Moroccan Footballer of the Year, he moved to Saudi Arabian club Al Hilal by special permission of King Hassan II.
◗ He won the Asian Cup Winners' Cup and Asian Super Cup in a single season with Al Hilal before leaving for Spain.

ABDELKRIM HADRIOUI Age: 25 Club: Benfica (Portugal)
◗ Hadrioui is an attacking left-sided defender.
◗ He provided the cross for the Raghib goal against Ghana which won Morocco's place in France '98.
◗ He made four appearances in the qualifying campaign.

KHALID RAGHIB

Age: 29 Club: Settat

◗ He secured Morocco's World Cup place with a goal against Ghana in June 1997.
◗ It was a header in front of 90,000 spectators.
◗ He scored three goals in three qualifying matches.

MANAGER PROFILE *HENRI MICHEL*

There will be few coaches in the 1998 World Cup as experienced as Frenchman Henri Michel. Capped 58 times by his country, and a veteran of the 1978 World Cup, he won three French Championships with FC Nantes. In 1982 he switched to coaching and led the French Olympic team to gold in the 1984 Los Angeles Games. He took charge of the French national side and led them to third place in the 1986 World Cup before switching back to club football with Paris St Germain in 1988. A short break followed before working with Cameroon in the 1994 World Cup. A spell in Saudi Arabia came next and then he moved to Morocco. France '98 will be his fourth finals – his third as a coach.

GROUP A

Scotland

ROAD TO FRANCE

Austria 0 Scotland 0 (31 July 1996)	**Latvia 0 Scotland 2** (5 October 1996)
Scotland 1 Sweden 0 (10 November 1996)	**Estonia 0 Scotland 0** (11 February 1997)
Scotland 2 Estonia 0 (29 March 1997)	**Scotland 2 Austria 0** (2 April 1997)
Sweden 2 Scotland 1 (30 April 1997)	**Belarus 0 Scotland 1** (6 June 1997)
Scotland 4 Belarus 1 (6 September 1997)	**Scotland 2 Latvia 0** (11 October 1997)

WORLD CUP RECORD

In the last 24 years Scotland have outstripped England with their World Cup qualifying successes – appearing in five finals to England's three, and that is reason enough for their fans to cheer. But the time has come for something more. It is a weary old fact – but all the same a fact – that in the seven finals in which they have played a part, Scotland have never been beyond the first round. There have been some good results and some stinkers – their experiences of Argentina in 1978 encapsulating the entire Scottish misfortune. They lost 3-1 to Peru, drew 1-1 with Iran and then beat eventual finalists Holland 3-2. This was the era of great Dutch football played by the likes of Haan, Neeskens, Rensenbrink and Krol and for Scotland the result was almost as good as winning the competition. The feeling persists that if they get past Round One the atmosphere will become heady – and who knows what might happen then?

MANAGER | *CRAIG BROWN*

PROFILE

Craig Brown has done the easy bit, reaching France, but the hard bit is still to come. Brown, the No. 2 to former coach Andy Roxburgh, took charge in 1993 and his promotion signalled a sensational rise for a man who was once a schoolteacher and has not played the game at the top level. Brown sends out teams to play in a fast British style and has fashioned a competitive and disciplined side from a base of players who, while proficient, do not boast exotic abilities. Brown has played on typical Scottish strengths, a tough man who evokes unfailing loyalty from his players.

KEY PLAYERS

COLIN HENDRY Age: 32 Club: Blackburn Rovers (England)
- He won a Premiership medal with Blackburn in 1995.
- He cost manager Kenny Dalglish only £700,000 when he moved back to Ewood Park after two years at Manchester City.
- A blond, fearsome defender, Hendry won his first Scottish cap in 1993 against Estonia.

JOHN COLLINS

Age: 29 Club: Monaco (France)

- Collins was the first British footballer to be transferred to the continent under the Bosman ruling, although Celtic valued him at £3 million.
- He is a free-kick specialist.
- He was born in the Borders town of Galashiels, known more as a Rugby Union stronghold.

KEVIN GALLACHER

Age 31. Club: Blackburn Rovers (England)

- Gallacher suffered two broken legs while at Blackburn, the second in his comeback match from the first injury which happened against Arsenal in 1994.
- He wears contact lenses and has played blind, having lost them while on the pitch.
- He was crucial to the qualifying campaign scoring seven goals to take Scotland to France '98.

GROUP A

Norway

ROAD TO FRANCE

Norway 5 Azerbaijan 0 (2 June 1996)	Norway 3 Hungary 0 (9 October 1996)
Switzerland 0 Norway 1 (10 November 1996)	Norway 1 Finland 1 (30 April 1997)
Hungary 1 Norway 1 (8 June 1997)	Finland 0 Norway 4 (20 August 1997)
Azerbaijan 0 Norway 1 (6 September 1997)	Norway 5 Switzerland 0 (11 October 1997)

WORLD CUP RECORD

The book on Norway's major international foot-balling exploits is not very thick – they played in the 1938 and 1994 World Cup finals and have never made the European Championship finals. Even so, the 1990s have coincided with a rise in their world status and they are a side expected to cause an upset or two. Back in 1938 in France, the World Cup was played in a straight knockout format and Norway went down 2-1 to Italy, the eventual champions, in the first round. In 1994 they played in a four-team group which finished with all sides boasting a win, a defeat and a draw, but a single goal scored and one goal conceded meant that Norway were eliminated on goal difference. Coach Egil Olsen has tightened up the side and used just 23 players in the eight qualifying matches. A record of six wins and two draws in qualifying marked them out as a team head and shoulders above the rest of their group.

MANAGER PROFILE — EGIL OLSEN

Egil Olsen is a man who believes in doing his homework – he has a comprehensive database on all his side's matches and directs his team to play in an efficient and effective manner. It has not made him popular, but ever a pragmatist, he realizes all-out attacking football comes at a price. Capped 16 times by Norway, Olsen coached the Norweigan Olympic team from 1979 to 1985, moved to run the Under-21s and then in 1990 was made national coach. Two World Cup finals and a near-miss on qualification for the 1996 Euro Championship have marked him out as a coach who can lead Norway to heights they have never previously reached.

KEY PLAYERS

JAHN IVAR JAKOBSEN   Age: 32 Club: Rosenborg

- Jakobsen is an all-action player but is relatively small, which has earned him the nickname 'Mini' with his international team-mates.
- He has won six Norwegian league titles with Rosenborg as well as three Norwegian Cups, most recently in 1996.
- He made his international debut against Bulgaria way back in August 1988 and has since won over 60 caps.

OYVIND LEONHARDSEN

Age: 27 Club: Liverpool (England)

- Leonhardsen won three consecutive Norwegian titles between 1992 and 1994 with former club Rosenborg before joining Wimbledon for £600,000.
- It was Leonhardsen's goal against Switzerland in Berne that put Norway top of Group Three during their World Cup qualifying campaign.
- He joined Liverpool in the summer of 1997 for £4.5 million, a move which saw him link up with England midfielder Paul Ince.

OLE GUNNAR SOLSKJAER

Age: 25 Club: Manchester United (England)

- Solskjaer made an immediate impact at Manchester United after signing from Molde FK and finished his first season as the club's leading Premiership scorer.
- His youthful appearance and natural goalscoring ability have earned him the nickname of the Baby-Faced Assassin, a title he is known to hate.
- He was born in the small fishing port of Kristiansund. His father Oivind is a former professional wrestler.

GROUP B

Italy

ROAD TO FRANCE

Moldova 1 Italy 3 (5 October 1996)	Georgia 0 Italy 0 (10 September 1997)
Italy 1 Georgia 0 (9 October 1996)	Italy 0 England 0 (11 October 1997)
England 0 Italy 1 (12 February 1997)	Italy 3 Moldova 0 (29 March 1997)
Poland 0 Italy 0 (2 April 1997)	Italy 3 Poland 0 (30 April 1997)
PLAY-OFF	
Russia 1 Italy 1 (29 October 1997)	Italy 1 Russia 0 (15 November 1997)

WORLD CUP RECORD

What was different about the 1958 World Cup? The answer: Italy did not play in it. Apart from the 1930 tournament this was the only one they have missed – although reaching France '98 was a close squeeze, Italy making it via a play-off with Russia. Italy are undoubtedly one of the great World Cup countries, with five appearances in the Final and three wins. Their last Final appearance was in America four years ago where they lost on penalties to Brazil.

They first collected the trophy in 1934 when they beat Czechoslovakia 2-1 in Rome thanks to a late equalizer which forced extra-time. Four years later Italy successfully defended their prize with a 4-2 win over Hungary. There was no doubt that with Ferrari and Meazza anchoring the side from midfield, Italy were the side of their era and were only prevented from claiming greater glory by the outbreak of the Second World War. They reached the 1970 Final in Mexico but were overwhelmed 4-1 by Brazil.

It was 12 years before their next Final – in Spain – carried there by stars like Conti, Tardelli, Gentile and Rossi. Three draws in the 1982 qualifying rounds led to an impressive second-round group where Argentina and Brazil were beaten. Poland were beaten 2-0 in the semi-final and then West Germany were crushed in the Final as Italy built up a cosy 3-0 lead. The defence of the trophy in 1986 ended when France won 2-0 in their last-16 clash while 1990 – played again on home soil – ended in a penalty shoot-out semi-final defeat by Argentina. America proved more fruitful as Nigeria, Spain and Bulgaria were beaten to set up a final with arch-rivals Brazil. A dull match ended 0-0 and went to penalties. When Roberto Baggio missed with Italy's fifth penalty, Brazil became the unofficial kings of World Cup football with four wins to Italy's three.

KEY PLAYERS

PAOLO MALDINI Age: 29 Club: AC Milan
- Maldini has played for Milan throughout his whole career, making over 350 appearances.
- His father, Cesare, is coach of the Italian national team and played 14 times for Italy.
- Maldini was voted World Player of the Year in 1994.

DEMETRIO ALBERTINI
Age: 26 Club: AC Milan
- He has won more than 50 Italian caps.
- Albertini played in all of Italy's World Cup final games in USA '94.
- He has won four championship and two European Cup medals.

GIANFRANCO ZOLA
Age: 31 Club: Chelsea (England)
- Zola learned his trade as a free-kick specialist under the tutorship of Maradona at Naples.
- He scored the goal that beat England at Wembley in February, jeopardizing their chances of qualifying.
- He won the 1997 Footballer of the Year award in England after less than one season with Chelsea.

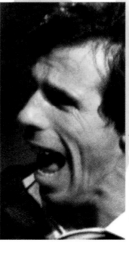

MANAGER	*CESARE MALDINI*

PROFILE

As a player, Cesare Maldini collected four championships and a European Cup with AC Milan, but despite this success won just 14 caps. He moved into coaching with Foggia, Terni and then Parma before being drafted in to help with the national side as an assistant to Enzo Bearzot, who masterminded the 1982 World Cup triumph. Maldini coached the Under-21 side to three European titles between 1992 and 1996 before he was asked to take Italy to the France '98 finals in December 1996.

GROUP B

Cameroon

ROAD TO FRANCE

Togo 2 Cameroon 4 (10 November 1996)   Cameroon 0 Angola 0 (12 January 1997)
Cameroon 1 Zimbabwe 0 (6 April 1997)   Cameroon 2 Togo 0 (27 April 1997)
Angola 1 Cameroon 1 (8 June 1997)   Zimbabwe 1 Cameroon 2 (17 August 1997)

WORLD CUP RECORD

The emergence of Africa as a continent with great footballing potential was signalled by the arrival of Cameroon on the world stage back in 1982. Prior to France '98 Cameroon had qualified for the World Cup finals three times and, bar a collapse in 1994, have distinguished themselves. Back in Spain at their debut finals, they drew 0-0 with Peru, 0-0 with Poland and 1-1 with Italy. This was not enough to take them through to the second stage, but by their next appearance, in Italy in 1990, they had come on in leaps and bounds. They stunned world football with a 1-0 win over defending champions Argentina and then saw off Romania 2-1. In the last 16 they beat Colombia 2-1 and were only knocked out in the quarter-finals by England, going down 3-2 in extra-time after conceding two penalties. In America four years ago they started with a 2-2 draw with Sweden, but a 3-0 defeat by Brazil led to a collapse in their spirit and they were hammered 6-1 by Russia in the final group match.

KEY PLAYERS

PATRICK MBOMA Age: 27 Club: Gamba Osaka (Japan)

▶ Mboma's family emigrated from Douala, Cameroon, to France when Mboma was two years old.
▶ He started his career with Chateauroux, later joining Paris St Germain and Metz.
▶ He obtained a French passport, but six goals for Cameroon made him leading scorer in the World Cup qualifying tournament.

SALOMAN OLEMBE Age: 17 Club: Nantes (France)

▶ He became the youngest opponent ever to face England in a senior Wembley international when introduced as substitute during a 2-0 defeat in November, at the age of 16 years 342 days.
▶ Olembe wears size six boots.
▶ When he appeared against England he had played only three first-team matches for Nantes, who were so eager to protect their prodigy they sent a party of escorts to whisk him back to France immediately after the match.

JACQUES SONGO'O

Age: 33 Club: Deportivo La Coruna (Spain)

▶ Songo'o made his Cameroon debut against Angola in the 1983 Olympic qualifier.
▶ His only appearance in two World Cup finals series was a 6-1 defeat by Russia in San Francisco.
▶ He spent five years in France playing for Toulon, Le Mans and Metz.

MANAGER	*JEAN MANGA ONGUENE*

PROFILE

Jean Manga Onguene was the assistant to Valeri Nepomniachi, who was at the helm for the successful 1990 campaign. Onguene took charge in July 1997 having served a thorough apprenticeship. An international with a career spanning 14 years from 1966–80, he played for Canon Yaounde and, after retiring, earned a coaching badge before joining the national team staff and progressing through the ranks.

GROUP B

Austria

ROAD TO FRANCE

Austria 0 Scotland 0 (31 August 1996)
Austria 2 Latvia 1 (9 November 1996)
Austria 2 Estonia 0 (30 April 1997)
Estonia 0 Austria 3 (20 August 1997)
Belarus 0 Austria 1 (10 September 1997)

Sweden 0 Austria 1 (9 October 1996)
Scotland 2 Austria 0 (2 April 1997)
Latvia 1 Austria 3 (9 June 1997)
Austria 1 Sweden 0 (6 September 1997)
Austria 4 Belarus 0 (11 October 1997)

WORLD CUP RECORD

In the beginning Austria were a feared world power in football. One of the 13 nations invited to contest the first competition, they reached the semi-final of the 1934 World Cup where they lost 1-0 to Italy. Then in a play-off for third place they were beaten 3-2 by Germany. By the time Austria next appeared in the finals they had to do it via qualifying. Once in Switzerland in 1954 they did their stuff, coming through the first round at a canter to meet the host nation in what must be one of the most remarkable World Cup matches ever. The score after 90 minutes: Austria 7 Switzerland 5. In the semi-final Austria lost 6-1 to Germany, but picked up third place via the play-off when they defeated Uruguay 3-1. Four years later they were on the plane back home from Sweden after failing to get through the first round.

There followed 20 years in the wilderness before a return to the finals stage in Argentina in 1978, where they reached the second round. Here they were outclassed 5-1 by Holland and lost 1-0 to Italy before saving face with a 3-2 win over rivals West

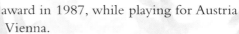

Germany. Spain, in 1982, saw them reach the second stage again, but a 1-0 defeat by France and a 2-2 draw with Northern Ireland ended their interest. Hosts Italy beat them 1-0 in 1990 and the Austrians also lost by the same score to Czechoslovakia. The only consolation was a 2-1 win over the USA.

KEY PLAYERS

TONI POLSTER

Age: 33 **Club:** FC Cologne (Germany)

- Depending on the number of friendlies played by Austria before the World Cup finals, Polster is on course to break Gerhard Hanappi's record of 93 appearances during France '98.
- He is the greatest Austrian goalscorer of all time, with 41 goals in 87 appearances.
- He won the European Golden Boot award in 1987, while playing for Austria Vienna.

ANDREAS HERZOG

Age: 29 **Club:** Werder Bremen (Germany)

- Herzog was signed by Werder from Bayern Munich in 1996.
- He had an operation on a recurring toe injury in October 1997.
- He scored the crucial goals in both Austria's 1-0 qualifying victories over Sweden.

MICHAEL KONSEL

Age: 35 **Club:** Roma (Italy)

- Konsel was sent off during a World Cup qualifier v Sweden.
- He spent 12 years with Rapid Vienna, winning consecutive League Championships in 1987 and 1988.
- He has been voted the most consistent keeper in Italy's Serie A.

MANAGER	*HERBERT PROHASKA*

PROFILE Herbert Prohaska was appointed in 1993 but it was too late to squeeze Austria through to the last World Cup. But he has made it for France and has a talented squad to hand. Prohaska, a player with Inter Milan and AS Roma in the late 1970s, has earned a reputation for producing exciting football teams. He has also coached Austria Vienna.

GROUP B

Chile

ROAD TO FRANCE

Venezuela 1 Chile 1 (2 June 1996)
Colombia 4 Chile 1 (1 September 1996)
Chile 1 Uruguay 0 (12 November 1996)
Peru 2 Chile 1 (12 January 1997)
Chile 6 Venezuela 0 (29 April 1997)
Chile 4 Colombia 1 (5 July 1997)
Uruguay 1 Chile 0 (20 August 1997)
Chile 4 Peru 0 (12 October 1997)

Chile 4 Ecuador 1 (6 July 1996)
Paraguay 2 Chile 1 (9 October 1996)
Argentina 1 Chile 1 (15 December 1996)
Bolivia 1 Chile 1 (12 February 1997)
Ecuador 1 Chile 1 (8 June 1997)
Chile 2 Paraguay 1 (20 July 1997)
Chile 1 Argentina 2 (10 September 1997)
Chile 3 Bolivia 0 (16 November 1997)

WORLD CUP RECORD

Invited to the first party in 1930, it was to be another 20 years and the World Cup of 1950 in Uruguay before Chile reappeared. Their interest did not last that long; they were beaten 2-0 by England and Spain. It was different in 1962 when Chile were hosts. They scored impressive group wins over Switzerland, beaten 3-1, and Italy, defeated 2-0. Then in the quarter-finals the USSR were sent packing 2-1 before Chile faced Brazil. The home team went down 4-2 but regrouped to win the play-off with Yugoslavia for a best-ever finish of third. In England in 1966 they disappeared without a whimper and the same happened in West Germany in 1974. It was to be eight years before their next qualification – this time in Spain where they lost all three of their group matches. France '98 represents Chile's first finals for 16 years.

MANAGER	*NELSON ACOSTA*

Nelson Acosta was born in Uruguay and featured in local football before taking on a coaching job with Fernandez Vial de Concepcion. He progressed to Chile and Union Espanola and was made Chilean coach at the start of the qualifying campaign for France '98. A man who favours counter-attacking as his chief tactic, he is blessed with two of the best strikers in the world, Marcelo Salas and Ivan Zamorano.

KEY PLAYERS

SEBASTIAN ROZENTAL

Age: 21 **Club:** Glasgow Rangers (Scotland)

◆ Rozental made his debut for Chile aged just 17 and became a regular in the team, until injury prevented him from playing for much of the 1996-97 season.

◆ He signed for Glasgow Rangers in a £4 million deal in January 1997 and impressed everyone with his skill and pace before twisting his knee on his home debut against St Johnstone.

◆ He could prove to be one of the surprises of France '98.

MARCELO SALAS

Age: 22 **Club:** River Plate (Argentina)

◆ Salas scored in the 3-0 victory over Bolivia that secured Chile's place at France '98.

◆ He has already become an automatic choice up front for his country and delighted fans with a first-half hat-trick in the 4-1 victory over Colombia.

◆ He became the target of a number of top European teams, with Lazio winning the race to sign him.

IVAN ZAMORANO 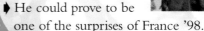 **Age:** 30 **Club:** Inter Milan (Italy)

◆ Zamorano has paired up with Salas to form a formidable striking force for the Chilean team.

◆ Not only a provider for Salas, Zamorano is also a lethal finisher in his own right, scoring five in the 6-0 victory over Venezuela.

◆ After winning the Spanish championship with Real Madrid, he moved to Inter Milan in 1996.

GROUP C

France

WORLD CUP RECORD

The time has come, they feel in France, for the cockerel to strut on the Final stage. Three times France have reached the semi-finals, and three times they have failed to go any further. The first time was back in 1958 when they faced mission impossible – a clash with Brazil. They lost 5-2 but recovered to win the third-place play-off against West Germany 6-3.

There were some barren years, but then in the 1980s, inspired by the remarkable Michel Platini, France became a force. They won the European Championship in 1984, two years after reaching their second World Cup semi-final. The 1982 tournament in Spain saw France recover from a 3-1 group defeat by England to beat Austria and Northern Ireland for a semi-final with West Germany. A cracking match ended 3-3 and went to penalties. Germany, as they have done so many times down the years, won it 5-4 and the crushed French then lost 3-2 in the play-off with Poland.

Mexico in 1986 saw France sail through the group stage for a knockout run that was, on paper, awesome. In the last 16 they faced Italy – and beat them 2-0. Then in the quarter-final Brazil – and beat them 4-3 on penalties after a 1-1 draw. West Germany were next, but France caught a cold and were beaten 2-0. Disappointed and with a squad that was getting old, France went into decline, failing to make Italy and the USA. Aime Jacquet, however, has sorted it out and got France playing again. They went through a 30-match unbeaten run and then reached the semi-finals of Euro '96 in England, where they were beaten by the Czech Republic.

Disappointing though that was, France have restored their confidence and, spurred by national expectation and no little skill, have become leading contenders to win the World Cup in their own backyard – a feat that used to be commonplace but has not happened since Argentina in 1978.

KEY PLAYERS
IBRAHIM BA

Age: 25 **Club:** AC Milan (Italy)

▶ He bleaches his hair in honour of his sporting hero, basketball star Dennis Rodman.

▶ He was handed the awesome responsibility in the 1997–98 season of replacing the legendary Franco Baresi at AC Milan.

▶ He was born in Senegal, where his father was an international player.

DIDIER DESCHAMPS

Age: 29 **Club:** Juventus (Italy)

▶ Eric Cantona called him 'the water carrier' because of his amazing stamina.

▶ He is the midfield anchorman, scoring only 16 goals in 12 seasons with Nantes, Marseille, Bordeaux and Juventus.

▶ He is one of the few players to have won the European Cup with different clubs – Marseille in 1993 and Juventus in 1996.

ZINEDINE ZIDANE

Age: 26 **Club:** Juventus (Italy)

▶ Dennis Bergkamp rates him the best player in Europe.

▶ Zidane was the midfield general behind Juventus reaching the 1996 and 1997 Champions' League Finals.

▶ He was blamed for France's failure in Euro '96 after a series of below-par performances.

MANAGER

PROFILE

AIME JACQUET

As a player Aime Jacquet won just two French caps – hardly a wealth of international experience. But he proved himself at club level with AS Saint-Etienne where, in a 12-year career, the club won five championships and three French Cups. His coaching career started with Olympique Lyonnais, then moved on to Bordeaux, Montpellier and Nancy. He led Bordeaux to three French titles. Appointed to the national coaching squad in the 1992–93 season, 56-year-old Jacquet succeeded Gerard Houllier in December 1993.

GROUP C

Saudi Arabia

ROAD TO FRANCE

Saudi Arabia 2 Kuwait 1 (14 September 1997) Iran 1 Saudi Arabia 1 (19 September 1997)
China 1 Saudi Arabia 0 (3 October 1997) Saudia Arabia 1 Qatar 0 (11 October 1997)
Kuwait 2 Saudi Arabia 1 (17 October 1997) Saudi Arabia 1 Iran 0 (24 October 1997)
Saudi Arabia 1 China 1 (6 November 1997) Qatar 0 Saudi Arabia 1 (12 November 1997)

WORLD CUP RECORD

Saudi Arabia reached their first World Cup finals in the USA in 1994, but they were far from nervous debutants. Drawn in Group F along with Holland, Belguim and Morocco, Saudi proceeded to do well enough to reach the last 16. They were beaten 2-1 in their first finals match – by Holland – but then upset Morocco 2-1 and secured their place in the knockout rounds with an impressive 1-0 victory over Belgium. The next match was against Sweden and they were comprehensively beaten 3-1 by a side destined to reach the semi-finals and then win the 3rd-place Final. Football was not played in Saudi Arabia until the late 1950s, when it was imported by European immigrants moving there to work in the booming oil industry. Developed with the help of Brazilian coaches, the country did not entertain World Cup hopes until 1978. Their performance in the USA was very much against the odds.

MANAGER PROFILE

ALBERTO PARREIRA

Alberto Parreira is a winner. He was in charge of Brazil when they won in the USA four years ago. This time he goes to the World Cup determined to enjoy the experience and with reaching the second round his main aim. Qualification was won by Otto Pfister, a German who has been in Africa for the majority of his coaching life, working his way up to bigger and better things. Pfister coached Rwanda, Burkina-Faso, Senegal, the Ivory Coast, Zaire and Ghana. He took Ghana to the final of the 1992 African Nations Cup, and was only appointed by Saudi in 1997.

KEY PLAYERS

KHALIL AL MUWALID

Age: 26 **Club:** Al Ahli

▶ He has 86 caps.
▶ He scored the crucial penalty in the 1996 Asian Cup Final against United Arab Emirates.
▶ He has a reputation for being a midfield dynamo.

HUSSAIN SULIMANI

Age: 20 **Club:** Al Ahli

▶ He was sent off for handball in the 86th minute of the 1996 Asian Cup Final.
▶ Sulimani already has 35 caps under his belt.
▶ He is the youngest player in the squad and is reputedly his manager's favourite.

MOHOMMED AL-DAEYEA

Age: 25 **Club:** Al Tae

▶ He has 89 caps.
▶ He kept Saudia Arabia in the Asian Cup Final with some brilliant saves.
▶ He was beaten three times in a friendly with Germany in February '97.

GROUP C

Denmark

ROAD TO FRANCE

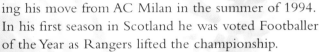

Slovenia 0 Denmark 2 (1 September 1996)	Denmark 2 Greece 1 (9 October 1996)
Croatia 1 Denmark 1 (29 March 1997)	Denmark 4 Slovenia 0 (30 April 1997)
Denmark 2 Bosnia 0 (8 June 1997)	Bosnia 3 Denmark 0 (20 August 1997)
Denmark 3 Croatia 1 (10 September 1997)	Greece 0 Denmark 0 (11 October 1997)

WORLD CUP RECORD

It is strange, given the international reputation of some of their players – the likes of the Laudrup brothers, Brian and Michael, and goalkeeper Peter Schmeichel – that Denmark have only once reached the finals of the World Cup, back in 1986. They started off in Mexico that year like a team possessed, romping through their group matches with a 1-0 win over Scotland, 6-1 over Uruguay and 2-0 over eventual finalists Germany. It then went wrong in the last 16 as Spain demolished them 5-1. Since then Denmark have been in the wilderness of world football, with one exception. Invited to join the 1992 European Championship at late notice, they then went on to win the competition. With a growing belief in their abilities and with players making waves in European football, Denmark have the potential to make a serious challenge and will be a side watched warily by all others.

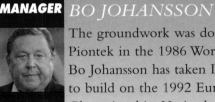

MANAGER *BO JOHANSSON*

The groundwork was done by Sepp Piontek in the 1986 World Cup finals, but Bo Johansson has taken Denmark forward, to build on the 1992 European

PROFILE Championship. He is obviously not afraid of learning from anyone – in 1996 Johansson brought his entire backroom staff over to England to watch Wimbledon in action. His challenge in France will start at the back with the commanding presence of Peter Schmeichel in goal, and that should give the defence plenty of confidence. From there his side have plenty of skill with the Laudrup brothers, particularly Michael who, although fast heading towards his mid-thirties, is still performing.

KEY PLAYERS

BRIAN LAUDRUP

Age: 29 **Club:** Chelsea (England)

▶ Laudrup has played top-flight club football in four European countries so far– Denmark, Germany, Italy and Scotland.

▶ He proved an instant hit at Rangers following his move from AC Milan in the summer of 1994. In his first season in Scotland he was voted Footballer of the Year as Rangers lifted the championship.

▶ He ended his self-imposed exile from the national team in time to be a part of the Denmark side which won the 1992 European Championship in Sweden.

MICHAEL LAUDRUP

Age: 33 **Club:** Ajax (Holland)

▶ Like father Finn and younger brother Brian, Michael is a Denmark international and the country's Footballer of the Year.

▶ He is the one surviving member of Denmark's only previous trip to the World Cup finals. Back in 1986, he scored one of the tournament's most memorable goals in the 6-1 drubbing of Uruguay.

▶ A dispute with then Denmark coach Richard Moller Nielsen led to him missing 29 internationals, including the 1992 European Championship.

PETER SCHMEICHEL **Age:** 34 **Club:** Manchester United (England)

▶ Schmeichel has won English championships and FA Cups since moving to Manchester United from Brondby in the summer of 1991.

▶ He played a key role in Denmark's greatest moment, their 2-0 European Championship final success over Germany in Sweden in 1992.

▶ He won his 97th cap for Denmark in the vital 0-0 draw in Greece, which ensured qualification for France '98.

GROUP C

South Africa

ROAD TO FRANCE

Malawi 0 South Africa 1 (1 June 1996)
South Africa 3 Malawi 0 (15 June 1996)
South Africa 1 Zaire 0 (9 November 1996)
Zambia 0 South Africa 0 (12 January 1997)
Congo 2 South Africa 0 (6 April 1997)
Zaire 1 South Africa 2 (27 April 1997)
South Africa 3 Zambia 0 (8 June 1997)
South Africa 1 Congo 0 (17 August 1997)

WORLD CUP RECORDS

This is South Africa's first appearance in the World Cup finals, but it comes as no surprise given the surge of African football in the last 12 years. Along with Cameroon and Nigeria, South Africa breathe fresh life into the tournament and will play with an innocence that could catch some of the established powers off guard. There is no telling what they will achieve, although given the successes of other African nations, there will be a sense of trepidation from their rivals. The best yardstick for measuring their advance is the fact that on their first entry into the African Nations Cup, they won the competition, beating Tunisia 2-0 in Johannesburg back in 1996. They were far from disgraced when they lost 2-1 against England at Old Trafford in 1997.

MANAGER *PHILIPPE TROUSSIER*

PROFILE Troussier was unable to start his job until the March before the '98 finals, but believed he could bring fresh blood to South Africa. He has managed Ivory Coast, Nigeria, Burkina Faso and was in charge of the South African club side Kaizer Chiefs for nine months in 1994. French born, he saw out his contract with Burkina before moving on to his World Cup duties.

KEY PLAYERS

MARK FISH

Age: 24 **Club:** Bolton (England)

◆ Fish became Bolton's joint record signing when he joined the Wanderers for £2.5 million from Lazio in August 1996.

◆ He was South Africa's youngest cap when he played against Mexico in October 1993, at the age of only 19.

◆ His hero is Marcel Desailly, whom he played alongside when he was chosen to appear in a FIFA World XI team against Brazil two years ago.

PHILOMEN MASINGA   **Age:** 28 **Club:** Bari (Italy)

◆ Masinga spent two years with Leeds United, scoring ten goals and earning the nickname of 'Waltzing Masinga'.

◆ He had a brief 'retirement' from international football, upset that he had been abused by home fans.

◆ He scored four goals in South Africa's World Cup qualifying campaign, including the goal against Congo which booked their passage to France.

JOHN MOSHOEU

Age: 32 **Club:** Kocaelispor (Turkey)

◆ Moshoeu's bicycle kick set up Masinga's goal when the South Africans played England at Old Trafford. Such tricks have brought him the nickname of 'Shoes'.

◆ He helped his club to a shock victory in the 1997 Turkish Cup, earning them a place in Europe.

◆ Moshoeu started his career at Blackpool; not the English Second Division club but his local team in Dobsonville, Johannesburg.

GROUP D

Nigeria

ROAD TO FRANCE

Nigeria 2 Burkina Faso 0 (9 November 1996) Kenya 1 Nigeria 1 (12 January 1997)
Nigeria 2 Guinea 1 (5 April 1997) Burkina Faso 1 Nigeria 2 (27 April 1997)
Nigeria 3 Kenya 0 (7 June 1997) Guinea 1 Nigeria 0 (17 August 1997)

WORLD CUP RECORD

The coming face of soccer, Nigeria have only once reached the finals – in 1994 – where they made the last 16 before losing 2-1 to Italy in extra-time. They reached that stage after beating Greece 2-0 and eventual semi-finalists Bulgaria 3-0 in the group rounds in America. That is not a bad record, and a further reason for expecting great things of Nigeria is the fact that they are the current Olympic champions, beating Argentina in the 1996 Final. That tournament was geared towards young players and it suggests that there is a considerable amount of emerging talent in the country. There have been triumphs on their own continent with two wins in the African Nations Cup: Nigeria beat Algeria in 1980 and Zambia in 1994.

MANAGER
BORA MILUTINOVIC

PROFILE

After much speculation and with Terry Venables' name in the frame, Nigeria eventually plumped for sacked Mexico coach Bora Milutinovic. He has done wonders with countries ranked as outsiders. As a player, Serbian-born Bora played for Partizan Belgrade before continuing his career in Switzerland, France and then Mexico, where he moved into coaching after his playing days ended. He was in charge of Mexico in 1986 when they reached the quarter-finals and he was at the helm of the USA side which surprised everyone by making the last 16 in 1994. Milutinovic replaces Amadu Shuaibu who was the surprise choice to succeed the Dutchman Clemens Westerhof in late 1994.

KEY PLAYERS

DANIEL AMOKACHI Age: 25 Club: Besiktas (Turkey)

◗ When Everton beat Manchester United in the 1995 FA Cup Final, the game was broadcast live in Nigeria for the first time because Amokachi came on as a sub.
◗ His big break came when he went on a tour to Holland with Nigeria when he was just 17. Bruges spotted him and signed him from his hometown club Ranchers Bees.
◗ He was close to signing for Juventus in 1994, but the deal fell through and he had to join Everton, who gave him a three-year deal worth £2 million.

SUNDAY OLISEH

Age: 23 Club: Ajax (Holland)

◗ Oliseh left home at the age of 16 to join Belgian club FC Liege, where he was first noticed by Nigeria's coach Clemens Westerhof.
◗ In the 1994 World Cup, it was Oliseh's sloppy throw-in that allowed Italy to score the equalizer and prevent one of the tournament's biggest shocks.
◗ In the 1996–97 season, while playing with FC Cologne, he was named as the best defensive midfielder in the Bundesliga.

FINIDI GEORGE

Age: 27 Club: Real Betis (Spain)

◗ George was voted best player in Holland during his spell with Ajax, where he won three Championships and a Champions' League title.
◗ He left Ajax for Spanish side Real Betis because he found his club-mates at the Dutch club cold and aloof.
◗ George played in all Nigeria's matches in USA '94, scoring against Greece.

Finidi George - Nigeria 1994

GROUP D

Bulgaria

ROAD TO FRANCE

Israel 1 Bulgaria 2 (1 September 1996)	**Luxembourg 1 Bulgaria 2** (8 October 1996)
Cyprus 1 Bulgaria 3 (14 December 1996)	**Bulgaria 4 Cyprus 1** (2 April 1997)
Bulgaria 4 Luxembourg 0 (8 June 1997)	**Bulgaria 1 Israel 0** (20 August 1997)
Bulgaria 1 Russia 0 (10 September 1997)	**Russia 4 Bulgaria 2** (11 October 1997)

WORLD CUP RECORD

Bulgaria have appeared in six World Cup finals, the first in 1962, but it wasn't until the finals in the USA in 1994 that they finally managed to win a game. Having done so, however, they forged through to the semi-finals, eventually losing the third-place Final. The East Europeans have certainly made something of an impact in recent years, and with the likes of Letchkov and Stoitchkov in their ranks have one of the most potent attacking midfield pairings in world football. Back in 1986 they drew 1-1 with defending World Champions Italy in their first match and had another 1-1 draw in the next game against South Korea. A 2-0 defeat by eventual champions Argentina could not stop Bulgaria reaching the last 16 where they were beaten 2-0 by Mexico.

In America four years ago, Bulgaria were the tournament's shock side. Hammered 3-0 in their opening group match against Nigeria, they then beat Greece 4-0 and Argentina 2-0. They reached the quarter-finals after a 1-1 draw with Mexico was settled on penalties. Then they faced Germany and produced one of the shocks of the competition, beating the World Champions 2-1. Italy proved too strong in the semi-final, triumphing 2-1 – and in the 3rd-place Final, a disheartened Bulgarian side were hammered 4-0 by Sweden.

MANAGER / PROFILE · HRISTO BONEV

Success has come thanks to a few truly world-class stars finding themselves playing in the same generation. That, however, will soon be a thing of the past if Hristo Bonev has his way. The former Bulgarian striker, with an impressive international record of 47 goals in 96 games, was put in sole charge after Euro '96 and has worked hard to instal a team-ethic in his charges. Demanding fitness levels have been set while players have been carefully coached into a system that is functional rather than immediately dynamic.

KEY PLAYERS

TRIFON IVANOV Age: 32

Club: Rapid Vienna (Austria)

▶ Ivanov is a rugged and aggressive player and fully lives up to his nickname of 'Wolfman'.

▶ He succeeded Hristo Stoitchkov as the national captain after Euro '96.

▶ Ivanov has been a full international for a decade, making his debut against East Germany in 1988.

HRISTO STOITCHKOV Age: 32

Club: Barcelona (Spain)

▶ Stoitchkov refused to play for his country for over a year in protest at the sacking of national coaches Dimitar Penev and Hristo Bonev after a disappointing Euro '96 campaign.

▶ He began his second spell with Barcelona when he signed from Parma in 1996.

▶ He finished the 1994 World Cup finals with six goals, to win the Golden Boot award for the tournament's top scorer and was instrumental in Bulgaria's march to the semi-finals.

YORDAN LETCHKOV Age: 30

Club: Besiktas (Turkey)

▶ Letchkov was another of the senior Bulgarian players who had a year's self-imposed exile from international football in protest at the sacking of Penev and then Bonev.

▶ Like many of his international team-mates he plays outside Bulgaria and transferred from Marseille to Besiktas in July 1997.

▶ He became famous for his diving header in the quarter-finals of the 1994 World Cup in America, which helped knock Germany out of the competition.

GROUP D

Spain

ROAD TO FRANCE

Faroe Islands 2 Spain 6 (4 September 1996)	Spain 4 Malta 0 (12 February 1997)
Czech Republic 0 Spain 0 (9 October 1996)	Yugoslavia 1 Spain 1 (30 April 1997)
Spain 4 Slovakia 1 (13 November 1996)	Spain 1 Czech Republic 0 (8 June 1997)
Spain 2 Yugoslavia 0 (14 December 1996)	Slovakia 1 Spain 2 (24 September 1997)
Malta 0 Spain 3 (18 December 1996)	Spain 3 Faroe Islands 1 (11 October 1997)

WORLD CUP RECORD

They boast one of the most glamorous leagues in the world, yet at international level Spain have not really delivered. By and large Spain have disappointed in the finals, although they had good competitions in 1986 and 1994. A fourth place in 1950 was achieved in a four-group second stage, with the top two teams then contesting the Final. Spain lost 6-1 to Brazil, 3-1 to Sweden and drew 2-2 with Uruguay. Hosts in 1982, they struggled through to the second round-robin stage where they had to play West Germany and England. They lost 2-1 to Germany, the eventual finalists, and drew 0-0 with England. Mexico in 1986 was a great improvement. After an opening match 1-0 defeat by Brazil, Spain picked up the pace, thrashed Denmark 5-1 in the last 16 and were denied a semi-final spot when Belgium beat them on penalties after a 1-1 draw. In America four years ago a 2-2 draw with South Korea did not augur well, but was followed by a 1-1 draw with Germany and a 3-1 defeat of Bolivia. In the last 16 Switzerland were crushed 3-0, but Spain were knocked out 2-1 by Italy, quarter-final winners and eventual finalists.

MANAGER *JAVIER CLEMENTE*

PROFILE Spain are taking their World Cup very seriously, with coach Javier Clemente able to keep tabs on all his squad because they are involved exclusively in Spanish club football. Javier, a Basque who played for Athletic Bilbao, took up the national coaching job in 1992 after helping Spain to an Olympic gold football medal. Willing to call on young players, Javier – now in his mid-forties – has given the side hope and in return the team embarked on a long unbeaten run following the 1994 World Cup – so impressive that it lifted Spain to second place in the world rankings.

KEY PLAYERS

FERNANDO HIERRO

Age: 30 **Club:** Real Madrid

In Spanish 'Hierro' means 'iron', which is fitting considering the Real Madrid defender is Spain's most notorious hardman.

He was selected for the Spanish squad for the 1990 World Cup finals in Italy but he did not make a single appearance during the tournament.

Hierro has a £21 million contract with Real Madrid which will keep him at the Bernabeu until 2003 and is worth a healthy £1.5 million per year.

LUIS ENRIQUE **Age:** 28 **Club:** Barcelona

Luis Enrique is a genuinely versatile player and can operate in the back four or as an attacking midfielder.

He has a 1993 Spanish Cup and a 1995 Spanish League winner's medal, which he won with his former club Real Madrid, where he spent five seasons.

In a 1997 poll of Barcelona fans, over 70 per cent voted Luis Enrique as the club's 'most valuable player'.

RAUL GONZALEZ **Age:** 21 **Club:** Real Madrid

Raul made his Real Madrid debut in a 5-0 victory over Barcelona and scored his first senior goal for the club against arch-rivals Atletico Madrid – the club he played for as a child.

His greatest ambition outside football is to meet the King of Spain.

He missed out on Euro '96 because, aged 19, he was considered too young. He went to Atlanta instead to help defend Spain's Olympic football title.

GROUP D

Paraguay

WORLD CUP RECORD

Peru 1 Paraguay 0 (16 March 1997)	Colombia 1 Paraguay 0 (24 April 1996)
Uruguay 0 Paraguay 2 (2 June 1996)	Argentina 1 Paraguay 1 (1 September 1996)
Paraguay 2 Chile 1 (9 October 1996)	Paraguay 1 Venezuela 0 (12 October 1997)
Paraguay 1 Ecuador 0 (10 November 1996)	Bolivia 0 Paraguay 0 (15 December 1996)
Venezuela 0 Paraguay 2 (12 January 1997)	Paraguay 2 Peru 1 (12 February 1997)
Paraguay 2 Colombia 1 (2 April 1997)	Paraguay 2 Uruguay 1 (30 April 1997)
Paraguay 1 Argentina 2 (6 July 1997)	Chile 2 Paraguay 1 (20 July 1997)
Ecuador 2 Paraguay 1 (20 August 1997)	Paraguay 2 Bolivia 1 (10 September 1997)

WORLD CUP RECORD

Four times Paraguay have been in the finals of the World Cup, but they are still waiting to make a significant impact on the tournament. They were invited to the first competition back in 1930, but a 3-0 defeat at the hands of the USA ended their interest. In Brazil 20 years on, they were eliminated after the first round following a 2-2 draw with Sweden and then a 2-0 defeat by Italy. A trip to Sweden in 1958 has been Paraguay's only previous World Cup in Europe. They managed a 1-1 draw with Scotland and a 3-3 draw with Yugoslavia but were hammered 7-3 by France. Paraguay's best moment came in 1986 when a 1-1 draw with host nation Mexico, a 1-0 win over Iraq and a 2-2 draw with Belgium took them through to the knock-out stages for the first time. There they met England and were comprehensively beaten 3-0.

MANAGER — *PAULO CESAR CARPEGIANI*

PROFILE

A firm believer that attack is the best form of defence, Paulo Cesar Carpegiani is a Brazilian who played for Porto Alegre and then Flamengo. He was a member of the Brazilian squad that went to West Germany for the 1974 World Cup. Now in his late forties, he started his coaching career with Flamengo – winners of the 1981 World Club Championship when they beat Liverpool 3-0. He also won a Brazilian League title with the club.

KEY PLAYERS

FRANCISCO ARCE

Age: 26 **Club:** Gremio (Brazil)

▶ Arce started his football career as a promising midfielder, but is now one of the best right-backs in South America.
▶ He played at the 1992 Olympics in Barcelona.
▶ Only a penalty shoot-out defeat by Ajax in the World Club Champion-ship has prevented him from a clean sweep of club honours at Gremio.

CARLOS GAMARRA **Age:** 26 **Club:** Benfica (Portugal)

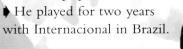

▶ He is the star man in the team's defensive back three.
▶ He was joint top-scorer with three goals in the World Cup qualification.
▶ He played for two years with Internacional in Brazil.

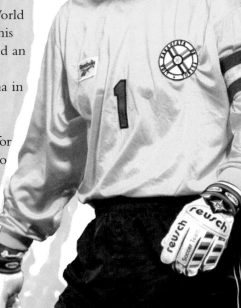

JOSE LUIS CHILAVERT

Age: 32 **Club:** Velez Sarsfield (Argentina)

▶ Chilavert is known as a flam-boyant and inspirational goalkeeper.
▶ During the World Cup qualifiers, his free-kick secured an important draw against Argentina in Buenos Aires.
▶ He received a four-match ban for fighting with Tino Asprilla in the match against Colombia in April 1996.

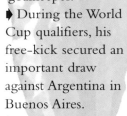

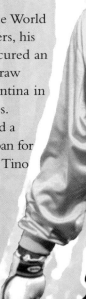

Mexico

ROAD TO FRANCE

Mexico 4 Canada 0 (2 March 1997)
Costa Rica 0 Mexico 0 (16 March 1997)
Mexico 6 Jamaica 0 (13 April 1997)
USA 2 Mexico 2 (20 April 1997)
Jamaica 0 Mexico 0 (16 November 1997)

Mexico 5 El Salvador 0 (5 October 1997)
Canada 2 Mexico 2 (12 October 1997)
Mexico 0 USA 0 (2 November 1997)
Mexico 3 Costa Rica 3 (9 November 1997)

WORLD CUP RECORD

Mexico have a long association with the tournament, dating back to the beginning in 1930, and have twice been quarter-finalists – both times when they have hosted the World Cup. They failed to qualify in 1934, 1974 and 1982, did not enter in 1938 and were banned in 1990, having played over-age players in an international youth tournament. Amazingly, it was not until the 1962 competition that they won a match in the finals stages, when they beat Czechoslovakia 3-1 in Chile. By that stage they had already lost to Brazil and Spain.

Mexico have a reputation for being an up-and-down side, brilliant against some of the best teams in the world and then dismal against outsiders – as in 1978 when they lost 3-1 to 1000-1 Tunisia. In 1970 they reached the last eight where Italy, the eventual finalists, needed extra-time to win 4-1. In 1986 it was West Germany, another country to progress past Mexico only to become beaten finalists, who triumphed – but only after penalties following a 0-0 draw. In the USA in 1994 Mexico reached the last 16 where they played Bulgaria. The match ended 1-1 but was decided in the Bulgarians' favour following a penalty shoot-out.

MANAGER *MANUEL LAPUENTE*

PROFILE

The hard work was done by Bora Milutinovic – a miracle worker who has done wonders with rank outsiders. He was in charge of Mexico in 1986 when they reached the quarter-finals and then the USA, where he took them to the last 16 in 1994. Back with Mexico, he helped them qualify for France – and was then fired after three poor results. Manuel Lapuente, coach of the Mexico City club Necaxa, is now in charge for the second time, having previously been fired in 1992.

KEY PLAYERS

JORGE CAMPOS

Age: 30 **Club:** Los Angeles Galaxy (USA)

▶ Campos helped Mexico win back-to-back CONCACAF Gold Cups in 1993 and 1995, finish runners-up in the 1993 Copa América and reach the last 16 of the 1994 World Cup.

▶ He is known as an 'overlapping goalkeeper' for his regular excursions upfield.

▶ He played most of the 1989 Mexican season as a striker because he could not dislodge the established goalkeeper at UNAM – and finished top scorer for the club with 14 goals.

RAMON RAMIREZ

Age: 27 **Club:** Guadalajara

▶ Without a doubt, Ramirez is the ball-winning fulcrum of the Mexican midfield.

▶ He made 14 qualifying appearances.

▶ He scored against Honduras and Canada as Mexico qualified

CARLOS HERMOSILLO

Age: 33 **Club:** Cruz Azul

▶ He made 14 appearances in Mexico's qualifying campaign.

▶ He scored 10 goals throughout the qualifying tournament.

▶ He ended this campaign two caps short of a century.

GROUP E

South Korea

ROAD TO FRANCE

South Korea 3 Kazakhstan 0 (6 September 1997)	**South Korea 2 Uzbekistan 1** (12 September 1997)
Japan 1 South Korea 2 (28 September 1997)	**South Korea 3 UAE 0** (4 October 1997)
Kazakhstan 1 South Korea 1 (11 October 1997)	**Uzbekistan 1 South Korea 5** (18 October 1997)
South Korea 0 Japan 2 (1 November 1997)	**UAE 1 South Korea 3** (9 November 1997)

WORLD CUP RECORD

In the last 12 years there has been something of a footballing renaissance in South Korea, who are making their fourth successive appearance in the World Cup finals. Until 1986 they had only reached the final stages once before – back in Switzerland in 1954. The Koreans will feel happy that time has made that memory fade, because they lost 9-0 to Hungary and then 7-0 to Turkey. The Hungary defeat was forgivable as it was against the Mighty Magyars; the Hungary of Puskás, Boszik and Kocsis.

By 1986 and the Mexico finals, South Korea had come on in leaps and bounds and they covered themselves with glory, if not winning results. They lost their first match 3-1 to Argentina, the eventual world champions, and drew 1-1 with Bulgaria before losing 3-2 to Italy. The results were not quite so good in Italy for the 1990 World Cup, where they lost all three of their group matches; beaten 2-0 by Belgium, 3-1 by Spain and 1-0 by Uruguay. The trip to the USA for 1994 was much better – there was a 2-2 draw with Spain, a 0-0 draw with Bolivia and a 3-2 defeat by Germany. They are still awaiting their first finals win, but given that they have run the footballing powers of Argentina, Germany and Italy close, the day must surely be close at hand.

MANAGER *CHA BUM-KUN*

PROFILE Appointed in January 1997 after ten seasons spent working in the German Bundesliga with Bayer Leverkusen and Eintracht Frankfurt, Cha Bum-kun has instilled German standards of efficiency, discipline, fitness and mental strength in his squad. Unbeaten in qualifying, a finals win would be a good enough starting point, but Bum-kun is more ambitious than that.

KEY PLAYERS

CHOI YOUNG-SU

Age: 24 **Club:** Sangmoo

◗ He was South Korea's leading scorer in World Cup qualification, netting eight goals.

◗ When South Korea played Japan in November, they lost after Young-su left the field with a nose injury.

◗ He featured in his country's Olympic team while playing with Lucky Goldstar Cheetahs.

PARK KUN-HA

Age: 26 **Club:** Suwon Bluewings

◗ He read a declaration of the Bluewings' intentions when they were formed and joined the Korean League in 1995.

◗ Kun-ha lists listening to music as his favourite hobby.

◗ His only goals of the World Cup qualifying campaign came in their 4-0 win over Hong Kong.

CHOI YOUNG-IL

Age: 31 **Club:** Pusan Daewoo

◗ He is one of South Korea's more experienced players, having played over 40 games for his country.

◗ He helped his club to a shock victory in the Adidas Cup.

◗ He enjoys watching all kinds of sport, especially NBA basketball.

Belgium

ROAD TO FRANCE

Belgium 2 Turkey 1 (31 August 1996)   **San Marino 0 Belgium 3** (9 October 1996)
Belgium 0 Holland 3 (14 December 1996)   **Wales 1 Belgium 2** (29 March 1997)
Turkey 1 Belgium 3 (30 April 1997)   **Belgium 6 San Marino 0** (7 June 1997)
Holland 3 Belgium 1 (6 September 1997)   **Belgium 3 Wales 2** (11 October 1997)
PLAY-OFF
Republic of Ireland 1 Belgium 1 (29 October 1997)   **Belgium 2 Republic of Ireland 1** (15 November 1997)

WORLD CUP RECORD

Belgium have been to the World Cup finals party nine times, yet boast a lowly FIFA world ranking of No. 48. They are always tough opponents, but it was not until the Spain World Cup of 1982 that they finally got beyond the opening round – where in a round-robin tournament they lost 3-0 to Poland and 1-0 to the USSR. Revenge was sweet in 1986, however, when they scored a thrilling 4-3 extra-time win over the USSR in Mexico.

In the quarter-final they were up against Spain, drew 1-1 and then triumphed 5-4 in the penalty shoot-out to win a semi-final place against the eventual winners Argentina. They lost the match 2-0.

Four years later they were in the last 16 again, having the better of the match against England. Extra-time was almost over when David Platt's spectacular volleyed winner ended Belgium's tournament in Italy.

In the USA four years ago, Belgium scored a superb group win over Holland, but then lost to Saudi Arabia. They qualified for the last 16 but faced Germany. Despite a good fight they were knocked out 3-2.

MANAGER *GEORGE LEEKENS*

PROFILE

A former Bruges defender, George Leekens learned his trade in Belgium, coaching at seven clubs – among them Anderlecht and Bruges. Now in his mid-forties, Leekens was put in charge of the national side early last year and guided them through to France '98 via a tough group and two tense play-off matches with the Republic of Ireland.

GILLES DE BILDE

Age: 26 **Club:** PSV Eindhoven (Holland)

▶ De Bilde was voted Belgian Footballer of the Year in 1994.

▶ He was banned for three months by the Belgian Football Federation after punching an opponent in December 1996.

▶ In just three months he was instrumental in PSV clinching the Dutch league title with a contribution of seven goals.

ENZO SCIFO

Age: 31 **Club:** Anderlecht

▶ Scifo has played for top European clubs including Anderlecht, Inter, Torino, Bordeaux, Auxerre and Monaco.

▶ He has Italian ancestry.

▶ In the mid-1980s he was Anderlecht's boy wonder.

MARC WILMOTS

Age: 28 **Club:** Schalke (Germany)

▶ Wilmots scored in the semi-final and final of Schalke's surprise UEFA Cup victory in 1997.

▶ He spent a lot of his boyhood helping his father farm the land north of Brussels.

▶ Before moving to the Bundesliga in 1996, Wilmots played for ten years in the Belgian league.

GROUP E

Holland

ROAD TO FRANCE

Wales 1 Holland 3 (5 October 1996)	**Turkey 1 Holland 0** (2 April 1997)
Holland 7 Wales 1 (9 November 1996)	**San Marino 0 Holland 6** (30 April 1997)
Belgium 0 Holland 3 (14 December 1996)	**Holland 3 Belgium 0** (6 September 1997)
Holland 4 San Marino 0 (29 March 1997)	**Holland 0 Turkey 0** (11 October 1997)

WORLD CUP RECORD

Until the 1970s Holland were one of the World Cup also-rans with just one appearance – in 1934. When they re-emerged in the 1974 World Cup in West Germany, they were to take football by the scruff of the neck and transform it into a pure game. Total Football was the Dutch way and with the likes of Haan, Krol, Neeskens, Rep, Cruyff, Rensenbrink and Van de Kerkhof, they had the players to make it happen. They strolled through the first group stages and played even better in the next super group round, beating Argentina 4-0, East Germany 2-0 and Brazil 2-0. That earned them a Final against the host nation, West Germany. Within a minute Holland led and they were clearly the better side. But dogged persistence brought Germany into the game and they lifted the trophy with a 2-1 win.

Four years later Holland still had too much for most opponents, and found themselves in a second group stage. A 5-1 win over Austria, a 2-2 draw with West Germany and a 2-1 win against Italy earned them a second successive Final – again facing the host nation, where they lost 3-1 in extra-time.

In 1990 they never really got going, but America proved a happier experience four years ago, until they went down 3-2 to Brazil, the eventual champions, in a pulsating quarter-final.

MANAGER PROFILE — GUUS HIDDINK

Guus Hiddink is true to the Dutch footballing philosophy of playing attractive football. Left with a difficult task of balancing players who are spread all around the globe, Hiddink has had to speak his mind to a group of them. Hiddink spent three seasons coaching Spanish league side Valencia and then had a spell at Fenerbahce. A close friend of Johan Cruyff, the former PSV Eindhoven player coached the Dutch club to the 1988 European Cup.

KEY PLAYERS

CLARENCE SEEDORF

Age: 22 **Club:** Real Madrid (Spain)

▶ A product of the successful Ajax youth policy, Seedorf made his international debut at the age of 18, against Luxembourg in 1994.

▶ He picked up a Champions' League winner's medal in 1995 with Ajax.

▶ He has already been the subject of two £3 million moves, firstly from Ajax to Sampdoria in Italy, and from there on to Real Madrid.

PATRICK KLUIVERT

Age: 21 **Club:** AC Milan (Italy)

▶ Kluivert became an instant sensation as a teenage striker for both Ajax and Holland. He scored the winning goal in the 1995 Champions' League Final.

▶ His double strike in the play-off qualification match against the Republic of Ireland sent Holland to the 1994 World Cup finals in the United States.

▶ He overcame personal problems and the pressures of a high-profile move to AC Milan to help his country again into the World Cup finals with two goals in the key qualifier against Belgium.

DENNIS BERGKAMP

Age: 29 **Club:** Arsenal (England)

▶ Bergkamp has won three European club medals in his career – two UEFA Cups (with Ajax and Inter Milan) and the Cup Winners' Cup with Ajax.

▶ He has a chronic fear of flying and vowed after the 1994 World Cup in the United States never to take to the air again.

▶ He joined Arsenal in July 1995 for £7.5 million and is the first player ever to win successive FA Carling Premiership Player of the Month awards.

GROUP F

Iran

ROAD TO FRANCE

ROUND ONE
Maldives 0 Iran 17 (2 June 1997)
Kyrgyzstan 0 Iran 7 (4 June 1997)
Syria 0 Iran 0 (6 June 1997)
Iran 3 Kyrgyzstan 1 (9 June 1997)
Iran 9 Maldives 0 (11 June 1997)
Iran 2 Syria 2 (13 June 1997)
Iran 0 Kuwait 0 (31 October 1997)
THIRD PLACE
Iran 2 Japan 3 (16 November 1997)
PLAY-OFF
Iran 1 Australia 1 (22 November 1997)

ROUND TWO
China 2 Iran 4 (13 September 1997)
Iran 1 Saudi Arabia 1 (19 September 1997)
Kuwait 1 Iran 1 (26 Sptember 1997)
Iran 3 Qatar 0 (3 October 1997)
Iran 4 China 1 (17 October 1997)
Saudia Arabia 1 Iran 0 (24 October 1997)
Qatar 2 Iran 0 (7 November 1997)

Australia 2 Iran 2 (29 November 1997)

WORLD CUP RECORD

Their one finals appearance before France '98 came in 1978, when Iranian football was at its strongest. They had just won their third Asian Championship in 1976, having held the title twice before, in 1972 and 1968. They went to Argentina and were in a tough group facing Holland, the eventual finalists, Peru and Scotland. They lost 3-0 to Holland and 4-1 to Peru but in between had their moment of glory, a 1-1 draw with Scotland. Encouraged, the next World Cup in Spain in 1982 became a real target, but revolution and war with Iraq pushed football out of the way. When they returned to the Asian Championship in 1988 they came third, a position not bettered – although their sensational play-off qualifying win over Australia, when they came back from 2-0 down in the last 20 minutes in Melbourne to make it 2-2 and qualify on away goals, marks a significant upturn in the fortunes of Iranian football.

MANAGER | TOMISLAV IVIC

PROFILE

A Croatian who has set his stall with a tough schedule for Iran after watching tapes of the qualifying games. Appointed in January 1998, 64-year-old Ivic was a player with Hajduk Split and at the end of his playing days started coaching, having worked in Belgium, Turkey, Italy, Greece, Portugal, Spain and France. After being put in charge of Iran, he ordered back-to-back training sessions and started to plan an 11-match build up to the World Cup finals.

KEY PLAYERS

ALI DAEI

Age: 29 **Club:** Arminia Bielefeld (Germany)

▶ Daei set up an internet site to petition his return to the national team after he was dropped as punishment.
▶ In 1996 he scored 22 international goals.
▶ He was picked last year for the Asian Select XI.

KARIM BAGHERI

Age: 24 **Club:** Arminia Bielefeld (Germany)

▶ He scored 17 goals in the World Cup qualifying rounds.
▶ He struck five times in Iran's 17-0 win over the Maldives.
▶ He plays in the German Bundesliga.

KHODADAD AZIZI

Age: 25 **Club:** FC Cologne (Germany)

▶ He scored the crucial equalizer against Australia in front of 120,000 fans in Tehran.
▶ He plays in the German Bundesliga, but turned down Borussia Dortmund because of the competition for places.
▶ He was voted Asian Footballer of the Year in 1997.

GROUP F

USA

ROAD TO FRANCE

Jamaica 0 USA 0 (2 March 1997)
Costa Rica 3 USA 2 (23 March 1997)
El Salvador 1 USA 1 (29 June 1997)
USA 1 Jamaica 1 (3 October 1997)
Canada 0 USA 3 (9 November 1997)

USA 3 Canada 0 (16 March 1997)
USA 2 Mexico 2 (20 April 1997)
USA 1 Costa Rica 0 (7 September 1997)
Mexico 0 USA 0 (2 November 1997)
USA 4 El Salvador 2 (16 November 1997)

WORLD CUP RECORD

The progress of football in America can be measured by their appearances in World Cup finals – and France '98 will be their third successive tournament. In 1994 they qualified as hosts, but they then surpassed all expectations by reaching the last 16 where eventual champions Brazil could only beat them 1-0. Their finest 90 minutes, however, came in 1950 when they beat England 1-0 in the Brazil finals. The USA did reach the semi-finals of the 1930 inaugural tournament, where they were thrashed 6-1 by Argentina, but then the invitation-only event was hardly representative of world football. Today, American footballers are emerging to play in other countries and from the 1994 experience, the likes of Alexi Lalas ended up in Italy, and Cobi Jones in the Premiership along with goalkeeper Kasey Keller.

KEY PLAYERS

KASEY KELLER Age: 28 Club: Leicester City (England)

◗ Keller captained 1996 US Olympic team and was runner-up in the 1997 US Player of the Year awards.
◗ He obtained a sociology degree by correspondence course after leaving Portland University to join Millwall in February 1992.
◗ He won a Coca-Cola Cup winner's medal as keeper for Leicester against Middlesbrough in April 1997.

MANAGER *STEVE SAMPSON*

PROFILE

Steve Sampson made his mark coaching in American University football, leading Santa Clara in California to the college title. From there he progressed to the US national side and was an assistant to Bora Milutinovic in the USA's 1994 World Cup campaign. Sampson was promoted after Bora moved south to take charge of Mexico for a second time.

JOVAN KIROVSKI Age: 20 Club: Borussia Dortmund (Germany)

◗ Kirovski was born in Macedonia but brought up in San Diego.
◗ Spotted by Manchester United when on a youth tour, he emigrated to England, scored more than a goal a game in the Old Trafford youth team and was top scorer with 20 goals as the reserves won the 1995–96 Pontins League.
◗ He was refused a British work permit and now plays in Germany.

PREDRAG RADOSAVLJEVOIC Age: 34 Club: Kansas City Wiz

◗ He scored 399 goals in 370 games over nine years in US Indoor soccer.
◗ He had spells at Everton and Portsmouth before returning to the US and becoming Kansas captain.
◗ Known as 'Preki', he was born in Belgrade and represented Yugoslavia before emigrating to the United States, for whom he scored in the 4-2 final qualifying win over El Salvador.

Yugoslavia

ROAD TO FRANCE

Yugoslavia 3 Faroe Islands 1 (24 April 1996)	**Yugoslavia 6 Malta 0** (2 June 1996)
Faroe Islands 1 Yugoslavia 8 (6 October 1996)	**Yugoslavia 1 Czech Republic 0** (10 November 1996)
Spain 2 Yugoslavia 0 (14 December 1996)	**Czech Republic 1 Yugoslavia 2** (2 April 1997)
Yugoslavia 1 Spain 1 (30 April 1997)	**Yugoslavia 2 Slovakia 0** (8 June 1997)
Slovakia 1 Yugoslavgia 1 (10 September 1997)	**Malta 0 Yugoslavia 5** (11 October 1997)

PLAY-OFF

Hungary 1 Yugoslavia 7 (29 October 1997)   **Yugoslavia 5 Hungary 0** (15 November 1997)

WORLD CUP RECORD

This will be only the fourth World Cup finals that Yugoslavia have played since 1974, although they did leave an impressive mark on Italia '90. In Italy they reached the quarter-finals where they lost to Argentina on penalties. The quarter-finals – also reached in 1958 – are not unfamiliar territory to Yugoslavia, who enjoyed their best competition in Chile in 1962. That year they recovered from a 2-0 group-stage defeat by the USSR, to sweep past West Germany 1-0 in the last eight before going down 3-1 to Czechoslovakia in the semis. They had reached the semi-finals of the first competition in 1930, but were thrashed 6-1 by eventual winners Uruguay. There was a gap of 12 years from the Chile tournament to Yugoslavia's next appearance in Germany, where the first round group stage was negotiated in some style – a 0-0 draw with Brazil, a 9-0 thrashing of Zaire and a 1-1 draw with Scotland. Then the wheels came off as in the next group stage Yugoslavia lost to West Germany, Poland and Sweden. The trip to Spain in 1982 was brought to a premature halt by the hosts.

MANAGER | *SLOBODAN SANTRAC*

PROFILE

Slobodan Santrac was a former player with OFK Belgrade and then in Switzerland with Grasshopper Zurich, Santrac won eight caps for Yugoslavia. He was put in charge of the national team in 1994 and his success in guiding them to France '98 was made sweeter by the emphatic way they came through the play-off with Hungary, winning 12-1 on aggregate.

PREDRAG MIJATOVIC Age: 29

Club: Real Madrid (Spain)

▶ He scored 14 goals in the World Cup qualifying matches.

▶ In the 1995–96 season he scored 28 goals for Valencia.

▶ Real Madrid paid £6.3 million for him in 1996.

VLADIMIR JUGOVIC Age: 28 Club: Lazio (Italy)

▶ Has won the European Champions' Cup with Red Star Belgrade (1991) and Juventus (1996).

▶ He has one of the most powerful shots from open or set play in the game.

▶ He has now played for three top Italian teams: Sampdoria, Juventus and Lazio.

DEJAN SAVICEVIC Age: 31 Club: AC Milan (Italy)

▶ He has won more caps than any of the other squad members, with the exception of Dragan Stojkovic.

▶ Savicevic has played nearly 100 games for Milan, scored 20 times and set up countless other goals.

▶ He scored in Milan's 4-0 victory over Barcelona in the 1994 European Cup Final.

GROUP F

Germany

ROAD TO FRANCE

Armenia 1 Germany 5 (9 October 1996)	**Ukraine 0 Germany 0** (7 June 1997)
Germany 1 Northern Ireland 1 (9 November 1996)	**Northern Ireland 1 Germany 3** (20 August 1997)
Portugal 0 Germany 0 (14 December 1996)	**Germany 1 Portugal 1** (6 September 1997)
Albania 2 Germany 3 (2 April 1997)	**Germany 4 Armenia 0** (11 September 1997)
Germany 2 Ukraine 0 (30 April 1997)	**Germany 4 Albania 3** (11 October 1997)

WORLD CUP RECORD

Only Brazil have won the competition more times than Germany, who have only missed the 1930 and 1950 World Cup finals.

The Germans won their first World Cup in 1954, upsetting the odds to triumph in Switzerland. In the Final against Hungary, the Germans were 2-0 down after eight minutes, but they would not give up and came back to win 3-2. They lost to England in the 1966 Final; won on home soil in 1974 when they beat Holland 2-1 after conceding a goal in the first minute; lost 3-1 to Italy in the Spanish World Cup of 1982; and four years later in Mexico went down 3-2 to Argentina.

They gained sweet revenge in 1990 when Andreas Brehme's penalty settled a dire Final in Italy where Germany won 1-0.

Defending their title in America, Germany reached the quarter-finals but were surprisingly knocked out by Bulgaria. As well as their past World Cup successes, Germany are also the holders of the European Championship – another trophy they have won three times.

MANAGER	BERTI VOGTS

PROFILE

The name of Berti Vogts is familiar and so it should be. Vogts was a playing legend for Germany – 96 caps, a World Cup winner's medal in 1974 plus considerable club success with Monchengladbach, including two UEFA Cups. He has done his time coaching, having been at the helm of the Youth and Under-20 teams before joining Franz Beckenbauer in preparing the 1990 World Cup-winning national side. Vogts then took charge, but his team were surprisingly beaten in America by Bulgaria. The coach, however, has since made amends with success in the 1996 European Championship, won in sudden-death overtime against the Czech Republic.

KEY PLAYERS

CHRISTIAN ZIEGE Age: 26 Club: AC Milan (Italy)

▶ Left-back Ziege, who began his career as a goalkeeper, has often been compared to international legend Andreas Brehme.

▶ He made his international debut against Brazil at the US Cup in 1993 and has been a regular in the German side ever since.

▶ His greatest achievement at club level was his part in Bayern Munich's victory in the 1996 UEFA Cup.

JURGEN KOHLER

Age: 32 **Club:** Borussia Dortmund

▶ One of the game's most respected defenders, Kohler is known as 'Ironfoot' in his native Germany.

▶ His involvement in Euro '96 was ended prematurely when he injured knee ligaments in Germany's first game of the tournament.

▶ Kohler actually retired from international football after Euro '96 but was persuaded to reconsider after leading Borussia to a 3-1 European Cup triumph over former club Juventus in 1997.

JURGEN KLINSMANN

Age: 33 **Club:** Tottenham (England)

▶ Klinsmann succeeded Lothar Matthaus as German captain for Euro '96 and led his side to victory in the Final against the Czech Republic, despite tearing a calf muscle earlier in the tournament.

▶ Klinsmann has already confirmed he will retire from international football after the World Cup.

▶ In his first season with Tottenham Hotspur, Klinsmann finished as the club's leading scorer and was voted Footballer of the Year.

GROUP G

Tunisia

ROAD TO FRANCE

Rwanda 1 Tunisia 2 (2 June 1996)	Tunisia 2 Rwanda 0 (16 June 1996)
Libria 0 Tunisia 1 (11 November 1996)	Tunisia 1 Egypt 0 (12 January 1997)
Namibia 1 Tunisia 2 (5 April 1997)	Tunisia 2 Liberia 0 (27 April 1997)
Egypt 0 Tunisia 0 (8 June 1997)	Tunisia 4 Namibia 0 (17 August 1997)

WORLD CUP RECORD

The North African country have made just one visit to the World Cup finals – back in Argentina in 1978, and they made a flying start. A 3-1 win over Mexico made them the group's leading side, following a 0-0 draw between the other two teams, West Germany and Poland. Beaten 1-0 by Poland, Tunisia got up off the floor to draw 0-0 with West Germany, the defending World Champions. However, their results – a win, a draw and a defeat – were not quite good enough to take them through because of Germany's 6-0 demolition of Mexico. After that Tunisian football took a back seat until 1996 when a successful World Cup qualifying campaign went hand in hand with a successful run in the African Nations Cup. They reached the Final where they lost 2-0 to South Africa.

KEY PLAYERS

MEHDI BEN SLIMANE Age: 24 Club: Freiburg (Germany)

◆ Ben Slimane was playing with AS Marsa in Tunisia when he went to the African Nations Cup, but when Tunisia reached the Final he was snapped up by Marseille.

◆ The weighty winger is nicknamed 'Dicker' at the German club Freiburg, where he moved in 1996.

◆ He scored once in the World Cup qualifying campaign, against Rwanda.

ADEL SELLIMI

Age: 25 Club: Nantes (France)

◆ He is Tunisia's most capped player, having made over 50 appearances for his national side.

◆ The left-sided attacker was Tunisia's leading scorer in World Cup qualification, with four goals.

◆ While with Club Africain in Tunisia, he won three Championships, one Turkish Cup and the African Club Cup in 1991.

MANAGER

PROFILE

HENRYK KASPERCZAK

Tunisians with a long memory might recall that their current coach Henryk Kasperczak was in the Poland team that beat them back in the World Cup finals of 1978. Kasperczak was a regular with Poland, playing in two World Cups, while his club football was with Metz in France. He later coached them to the French Cup before having spells with a number of other French clubs, among them Saint-Etienne, Strasbourg, Matra Racing, Montpellier and Lille. A five-month stint with the Ivory Coast – he took them to the semi-finals of the 1994 African Nations Cup – brought him to the attention of the Tunisian soccer authorities, who appointed him at the beginning of June 1994.

ZOUBIER BEYA

Age: 27 Club: Freiburg (Germany)

◆ The explosive midfielder joined his international team-mate Ben Slimane in Germany last season, leaving Tunisian club Etoile Sahel.

◆ He scored three goals on the road to France, including the only goal in the crunch match with Egypt.

◆ Beya, nicknamed 'Zouba' by the German fans, was one of the players of the tournament when Tunisia reached the Final of the 1996 African Nations Cup.

GROUP G

Romania

ROAD TO FRANCE

Romania 3 Lithuania 0 (31 August 1996)	Iceland 0 Romania 4 (19 October 1996)
Macedonia 0 Romania 3 (14 December 1996)	Romania 8 Liechtenstein 0 (29 March 1997)
Lithuania 0 Romania 1 (2 April 1997)	Romania 1 Ireland 0 (20 April 1997)
Romania 4 Macedonia 2 (20 August 1997)	Liechtenstein 1 Romania 8 (6 September 1997)
Romania 4 Iceland 0 (10 September 1997)	Ireland 1 Romania 1 (11 October 1997)

WORLD CUP RECORD

There was sweet revenge for Romania when they beat the Republic of Ireland at home and then, already qualified for France '98, held the Irish to a draw in the return fixture. This was the only point dropped by Romania in their qualifying campaign, and they are making their seventh appearance in the World Cup finals. Invited to take part in the first World Cup back in 1930 and appearing again in 1934 and 1938, Romania's best days have come in the 1990s. In Italia '90 they reached the last 16 where they were beaten 5-4 on penalties by the Republic of Ireland, and then in the USA four years ago they went one round better. Once again, however, they were undone by their failure in the penalty shoot-out. This time they drew 2-2 with Sweden in normal time and lost the shoot-out 5-4.

KEY PLAYERS

BOGDAN STELEA

Age: 30 **Club:** Steaua Bucharest

- This goalkeeper is the David James of Romania – making blinding saves one moment, dropping clangers the next.
- He saved a penalty from Roy Keane in a key qualifying game against the Republic of Ireland. He had needlessly conceded the spot-kick by bringing down Ray Houghton.
- He has earned a living in five countries: Romania (Dinamo, Steaua Bucharest); Spain (Mallorca); Belgium (Standard Liege); Austria (Rapid Vienna); and Turkey (Samsunspor).

GHEORGHE HAGI

Age: 32 **Club:** Galatasaray (Turkey)

- His incredible skills have earned him the nickname 'Maradona of the Carpathians'.
- Current Republic of Ireland manager Mick McCarthy swapped shirts with Hagi after they faced each other in Italia '90. 'He's the best I've played against – I couldn't get near him,' said McCarthy.
- He won more free-kicks than any other player in both the 1990 and 1994 World Cups and will retire from international football after France '98.

DAN PETRESCU **Age:** 29 **Club:** Chelsea (England)

- His hardest opponent was Ruud Gullit, later his manager at Chelsea. They clashed when Petrescu played for Foggia and Genoa in Serie A and Gullit was the star of AC Milan.
- Petrescu won four championships in Romania with Steaua Bucharest – who reached the 1989 European Cup Final, losing 4-0 to AC Milan.
- He is the embodiment of the 1990s wing-back; technically excellent moving forward but also able to defend. It was England coach Glenn Hoddle who first put Petrescu in that role.

MANAGER *VICTOR PITURCA*

PROFILE

The former Romanian Under-21 coach took charge in March when Iordanescu was relieved of his duties. Like his predecessor, Piturca was a player with Steaua Bucharest and has some act to follow after Iordanescu led Romania to their best ever finish in the finals in 1994. The qualifying route for France '98 was also a triumph with 37 goals scored and just 4 conceded. Piturca, who was jailed under the communist regime of Romania, for gambling, was only released on the intervention of the former dictator Ceausescu.

GROUP G

England

ROAD TO FRANCE

Moldova 0 England 3 (1 September 1996)	**England 2 Georgia 0** (30 April 1997)
England 2 Poland 1 (9 October 1996)	**Poland 0 England 2** (31 May 1997)
Georgia 0 England 2 (9 November 1996)	**England 4 Moldova 0** (10 September 1997)
England 0 Italy 1 (12 February 1997)	**Italy 0 England 0** (11 October 1997)

WORLD CUP RECORD

The glory year was 1966 – Geoff Hurst scoring the only hat-trick in a Final as England beat Germany 4-2 at Wembley in extra-time. Since then it has been a roller-coaster ride, with qualification failures punctuated by glimpses of success. In 1990 England came through the group stages to beat Belgium 1-0 with the last kick of the match. Next, Cameroon were beaten 3-2 in the quarter-final, again after extra-time, before a 1-1 draw in the semi-final against West Germany led to penalties and England losing 4-3. In 1986 they reached the quarter-finals where Argentina won 2-1 thanks to the infamous 'Hand of God' goal by Maradona.

In the 1990s England have rediscovered their form, reaching the semi-final of Euro '96 and winning a four-way tournament in France which also included Brazil and Italy. England did not play in their first World Cup finals until 1950 – when they were sensationally beaten by the USA. Four years later in Switzerland they reached the quarter-finals and were to do the same again in Chile in 1962. Failure to hang on to their trophy in 1970 led to a dark period when they failed to qualify for successive finals, in Germany and Argentina.

MANAGER *GLENN HODDLE*

PROFILE

Glenn Hoddle was appointed when Terry Venables announced he was standing down in 1996. Hoddle has made his mark on the team and moulded them in his playing image – gifted and full of passing movement. A stalwart with Tottenham and then Monaco, he moved into coaching with Swindon Town and was then snapped up by Chelsea. He made a considerable impression at the London club, and once Venables announced he was leaving the England job, Hoddle became the only acceptable candidate for his replacement.

KEY PLAYERS

ALAN SHEARER

Age: 27 **Club:** Newcastle United

▶ Shearer became the most expensive player in the world when he joined Newcastle from Blackburn Rovers for £15 million in July 1996.

▶ He finished Euro '96 as the tournament's leading scorer with five goals from five appearances.

▶ He was the Premiership's leading scorer for three consecutive seasons between 1994–95 and 1996–97, but missed most of the 1997–98 season with a serious ankle injury.

DAVID SEAMAN **Age:** 34 **Club:** Arsenal

▶ Seaman has been England's first-choice goalkeeper for the past four seasons.

▶ He was instrumental in England's progress to the semi-finals of Euro '96, saving a penalty in the group stages against Scotland and another in the quarter-final penalty shoot-out against Spain.

▶ He has won every English domestic trophy in his 12 years with Arsenal and also has a 1994 European Cup Winners' Cup medal.

DAVID BECKHAM

Age: 23 **Club:** Manchester United

▶ Beckham is famous for his long-range shooting and scored a spectacular goal from the half-way line on the opening day of the 1996–97 season against Wimbledon.

▶ He was voted the PFA Young Player of the Year in 1996–97

▶ Beckham has attracted a lot of attention because of his engagment to Spice Girl Victoria Adams.

GROUP G

Colombia

ROAD TO FRANCE

Colombia 1 Paraguay 0 (24 April 1996)	**Paraguay 2 Colombia 1** (2 April 1997)
Peru 1 Colombia 1 (2 June 1996)	**Colombia 0 Peru 1** (30 April 1997)
Colombia 3 Uruguay 1 (7 July 1996)	**Uruguay 1 Colombia 1** (8 June 1997)
Colombia 4 Chile1 (1 September 1996)	**Chile 4 Colombia 1** (5 July 1997)
Ecuador 0 Colombia 1 (9 October 1996)	**Colombia 1 Ecuador 0** (20 July 1997)
Bolivia 2 Colombia 2 (10 November 1996)	**Colombia 3 Bolivia 0** (20 August 1997)
Venezuela 0 Colombia 2 (15 November 1996)	**Colombia 1 Venezuela 0** (27 September 1997)
Colombia 0 Argentina 1 (12 February 1997)	**Argentina 1 Colombia 1** (16 November 1997)

WORLD CUP RECORD

Colombia have reached three World Cup finals, but 1990 was the first tournament that saw them progress beyond the first stage. Their first appearance was in 1962 in Chile, where they lost in the group stage to Yugoslavia and Uruguay, but managed an entertaining 4-4 draw with the USSR. In 1990 a 2-0 win over the United Arab Emirates and a draw with Germany was enough to take them through to uncharted waters – the last 16. There they faced another side new to this level of football – Cameroon. In the end Colombia were beaten 2-1 in extra-time. In 1994, having arrived in America as strongly tipped outsiders, they came apart at the seams. They were beaten 3-1 by Romania and 2-1 by the USA, before salvaging some pride with a 2-0 win over Switzerland. Many wondered how a country with such fabulous extrovert talents as Faustino Asprilla, Freddy Rincon, goalkeeper Rene Higuita and Carlos Valderrama could lose the plot so badly. There was talk of betting coups and the subsequent murder of defender Andres Escobar – the man who scored a disastrous own goal in the match with the USA – added to the rumours.

MANAGER | *HERNAN DARIO GOMEZ*

PROFILE

Hernan Dario Gomez was appointed after the 1994 World Cup. He played in Medellin, first with Independiente and then Atletico before becoming the coach to the Colombia Olympic team in 1993. Following this, he became the right-hand man to Francisco Maturana for the USA trip in 1994. The failure of the Colombians saw more change and Gomez promoted. He managed to bring his side through a long qualifying section and inspired them to pick up their game after a run of three defeats in February and April 1997 – by Argentina, Paraguay and Peru – which threatened to derail their drive for France.

KEY PLAYERS

FAUSTINO ASPRILLA

Age: 29 **Club:** Parma (Italy)

◗ Signed by Kevin Keegan for £7.5 million, Asprilla remained at St James' Park for a further year under Dalglish before moving to Italy.

◗ His most impressive performance for Newcastle was the hat-trick he scored in the 3-2 win over Barcelona.

◗ He was Colombia's top scorer in the qualification matches, hitting the target seven times, including a hat-trick against Chile.

FREDDY RINCON

Age: 31 **Club:** Corinthians of Sao Paulo (Brazil)

◗ Rincon is a veteran on the World Cup stage, having played for Colombia in both Italia '90 and USA '94.

◗ He has previously had spells in both Italy (Napoli) and Spain (Real Madrid), but prefers football in Brazil: 'You can enjoy yourself more on the field.'

◗ In Italia '90, he saved Colombia from elimination when he scored a late equalizing goal against Germany, finishing a stunning series of passes which had completely split the German team.

CARLOS VALDERRAMA

Age: 36 **Club:** Tampa Bay (USA)

◗ Another Colombian veteran, he won his 100th cap in August 1997 against Jamaica.

◗ He is famous for his bizarre hairstyle, a cascading blonde afro.

◗ He has twice been voted South American Player of the Year.

GROUP H

Japan

ROAD TO FRANCE

Japan 6 Uzbekistan 3 (6 September 1997)   **UAE 0 Japan 0** (12 September 1997)
Japan 1 South Korea 2 (28 September 1997) **Kazakstan 1 Japan 1** (4 October 1997)
Uzbekistan 1 Japan 1 (11 October 1997)   **Japan 1 UAE 1** (26 October 1997)
South Korea 0 Japan 2 (1 November 1997) **Japan 5 Kazakstan 1** (8 November 1997)
PLAY-OFF
Japan 3 Iran 2 (16 November 1997)

WORLD CUP RECORD

The Japanese have never played in the World Cup finals before, but their love of football cannot be denied. They have a thriving League system and money to support it – after all, Grampus 8 were the Japanese club with the financial clout to sign Gary Lineker when he wound down his career away from England. Japan won the 1992 Asian Cup, staged in Hiroshima, and a willingness to organize and house whatever tournaments are going, along with a restructuring of the leagues, has helped develop the game. So successful were Japan in hosting the World Club Championship back in 1980 that the annual match between Europe's best club side and South America's club kings has not been held anywhere else since. Japan's biggest step in giving football prominence will come in four years' time when they are the joint-hosts of the 2002 World Cup with South Korea. Japan is ready for top-class football.

KEY PLAYERS

KAZU MIURA Age: 30 Club: Verdy Kawasaki

♦ Miura played a season in Italy in 1994–95, taking a £1 million pay cut to join Genoa – just to add European football to his CV.
♦ He left Japan at the age of 15 to go to Brazil, the home of his hero Pelé, and was offered a professional contract with Santos.
♦ The pin-up of Japanese soccer scored 14 goals in the World Cup qualifying campaign – including two hat-tricks against Macao and one against Uzbekistan.

YOSIKATSU KAWAGUCHI

Age: 21 Club: Yokohama Marinos

♦ The Japanese No. 1 goalkeeper saved over 30 shots from the Brazilian team when they played in the 1996 Olympics.
♦ He learned his trade at the centre of Japanese school football, Shimizu Commercial Senior High, and then had offers from seven clubs.
♦ In 1995 he was voted the Japanese League's Rookie of the Year, after keeping five clean sheets in his first five League games.

HIDETOSHI NAKATA Age: 21 Club: Bellmare Hiratsuka

♦ Nakata has said that he would prefer book tokens to medals as prizes for winning football honours.
♦ He won an Asian Cup-Winners' Cup medal with Bellmare Hiratsuka in 1995.
♦ He had a spell training in Italy and wants to play abroad, seeing the World Cup as an opportunity to impress.

MANAGER / PROFILE

TAKESHI OKADA

Takeshi Okada was appointed in October 1996, replacing Shu Kamo as the national team manager, and he was able to give the country the lift needed to qualify for the World Cup finals. In his early forties, Okada has changed the pattern of play; his Japan are a fast-moving attacking side and, having qualified via a play-off, will be eager to show the world that they are not just in France to make up the numbers.

GROUP H

Croatia

ROAD TO FRANCE

Bosnia 1 Croatia 4 (9 October 1996)	**Croatia 1 Greece 1** (10 November 1996)
Croatia 1 Denmark 1 (29 March 1997)	**Croatia 3 Slovenia 3** (2 April 1997)
Greece 0 Croatia 1 (30 April 1997)	**Croatia 3 Bosnia 2** (6 September 1997)
Denmark 3 Croatia 1 (10 September 1997)	**Slovenia 1 Croatia 3** (11 October 1997)
PLAY-OFF	
Croatia 2 Ukraine 0 (29 October 1997)	**Ukraine 1 Croatia 1** (11 November 1997)

WORLD CUP RECORD

A state that only became a country in 1992 and was the focus for violent Balkan unrest, Croatia and Croatians see the football team as a means of bringing a united purpose to a newly-recognized country. The after-math led to 1,500 players leaving the country and reduced Croatian football to two professional clubs: Hadjuk Split and Croatia Zagreb. As a consequence, it has been difficult to sustain interest in local football, not just with the fans but with the players. Many have left to try their hand in other countries – among them Aljosa Asanovic, who spent some time at Derby County and is now at Benefica in Portugal, and Slaven Bilic who went to Everton via West Ham. Croatia's first major competition was Euro '96 in England.

MANAGER	*MIROSLAV BLAZEVIC*
PROFILE	

Miroslav Blazevic is nicknamed 'Attila' because of his short temper. Blazevic has marched around Europe gaining experience and saving money. He first worked as a coach in Switzerland, moved to Nantes in France before going to Greece, then returning to Croatia in 1993. The homecoming was to buy Croatia Zagreb – the club formerly known as HASK Gradjanski and then Dinamo Zagreb. He was appointed national team coach in place of Vlatko Markovic in March 1994.

KEY PLAYERS

DAVOR SUKER

Age: 30 **Club:** Real Madrid (Spain)

◗ Suker scored one of the most memorable goals of Euro '96 when he lobbed Denmark's Peter Schmeichel from an acute angle on the edge of the penalty area.

◗ He was top scorer for the Yugoslavia side which lifted the 1987 World Youth Cup.

◗ Suker's international record of nearly a goal a game is much better than his scoring rate in club football.

ALEN BOKSIC **Age:** 28 **Club:** Lazio (Italy)

◗ Boksic won the European Cup during his spell with Marseille in France in 1993, but narrowly failed to repeat the feat when his Juventus side lost the 1997 Final to Borussia Dortmund.

◗ He is currently in his second spell with Lazio, after originally joining them for £8 million.

◗ He was a member of Yugoslavia's World Cup squad at the 1990 finals in Italy, but did not play.

ROBERT PROSINECKI **Age:** 29 **Club:** Croatia Zagreb

◗ Prosinecki's pinpoint passing was a key feature in Red Star Belgrade's European Cup winning side in 1991.

◗ Now with Croatia Zagreb, the club which rejected him as a youngster, Prosinecki has played for both of Spain's premier clubs – Real Madrid and Barcelona.

◗ He won 15 caps for Yugoslavia and represented the country in the 1990 World Cup in Italy.

GROUP H

Argentina

ROAD TO FRANCE

Argentina 3 Bolivia 1 (24 April 1996)
Ecuador 2 Argentina 0 (2 June 1996)
Peru 0 Argentina 0 (7 July 1996)
Argentina 1 Paraguay 1 (1 September 1996)
Venezuela 2 Argentina 5 (9 October 1996)
Argentina 1 Chile 1 (15 December 1996)
Uruguay 0 Argentina 0 (12 January 1997)
Argentina 0 Uruguay 0 (12 October 1997)

Colombia 0 Argentina (12 February 1997)
Bolivia 2 Argentina 1 (2 April 1997)
Argentina 2 Ecuador 1 (30 April 1997)
Argentina 2 Peru 0 (7 June 1997)
Paraguay 1 Argentina 2 (6 July 1997)
Argentina 2 Venezuela 0 (20 July 1997)
Chile 1 Argentina 2 (10 September 1997)
Argentina 1 Colombia 1 (16 November 1997)

WORLD CUP RECORD

One of the great nations in the history of the World Cup, Argentina were there at the very beginning and were the first finalists, losing 4–2 to Uruguay. In 1958 they were beaten 6–1 in the group stage by Czechoslovakia and 3–1 by West Germany, but they fared slightly better in 1966 when they reached the quarter-final, only to lose 1–0 in a bad-tempered match with the eventual winners, England. By 1974 Argentina were developing, but the breakthrough was to come on home soil in 1978 when, inspired by Mario Kempes and current manager Daniel Passarella, they came through the first round as group runners-up but in the second group stage beat Poland 2–0, drew 0–0 with Brazil and then thrashed Peru 6–0. Facing Holland in the Final, Argentina won 3–1 in extra time, Kempes scoring twice.

A determined defence of their title ended at the second stage in Spain 1982, but they were back in force in 1986, with Maradona as the key figure. His controversial 'Hand of God' winner, which beat England 2–1 in the quarter-final, was followed by a 2–0 victory over Belgium to set up a Final with Germany which Argentina won 3–2. The defending champions made a dismal start in 1990, but soon regained their form to face Germany in the Final. Here, they gave the appearance of wanting to win the Cup by hanging on for yet another penalty shoot-out but were undone by a penalty conceded in the normal course of play. In America in 1994 they reached the last 16 but were knocked out 3–2 by Romania.

KEY PLAYERS

ARIEL ORTEGA Age: 24 Club: Valencia (Spain)

- Ortega is considered by many to be the best Argentinian player since Diego Maradona.
- Although only 23, he has already made over 30 appearances for his country and was practically an ever-present in the qualifying games for France '98.
- His £7 million transfer from River Plate was an Argentinian record.

GABRIEL BATISTUTA Age: 29
Club: Fiorentina (Italy)

- Batistuta was short-listed for European Footballer of the Year in 1997.
- He is a veteran at international level, having played over 50 games for Argentina, including the 1994 World Cup campaign.
- He joined Fiorentina in 1991 and, although the team got relegated from Serie A the following season, he stayed with them and helped them earn promotion.
- He has vowed to end his playing days at the club.

JAVIER ZANETTI Age: 23
Club: Inter Milan (Italy)

- Zanetti is a firm favourite with the Inter Milan fans for his tenacious work-rate and remarkably consistent performances.
- As a teenager, he was put a diet of beans, lentils and milk because he was so small and light. It worked.
- He was a member of Argentina's silver medal-winning team at the 1996 Atlanta Olympics.

MANAGER	DANIEL PASSARELLA

PROFILE

Daniel Passarella is one of the privileged few to have been summoned forward to collect the World Cup, having led Argentina to victory in 1978. Passarella became a giant of the game, a star in his home country with River Plate and then in Italy at Inter Milan and Fiorentina. Now in his mid-forties, he was appointed team coach in 1994 and guided his country through a long qualifying process, stabilizing the team after early disappointments including a 2–0 defeat by Ecuador and draws with Peru and Paraguay.

GROUP H

Jamaica

ROAD TO FRANCE

Jamaica 0 USA 0 (2 March 1997)	Mexico 6 Jamaica 0 (13 April 1997)
Canada 0 Jamaica 0 (29 April 1997)	Costa Rica 3 Jamaica 1 (11 May 1997)
Jamaica 1 El Salvador 0 (18 May 1997)	Jamaica 1 Canada 0 (7 September 1997)
Jamaica 1 Costa Rica 0 (14 September 1997)	USA 1 Jamaica 1 (3 October 1997)
El Salvador 2 Jamaica 2 (9 November 1997)	Jamaica 0 Mexico 0 (16 November 1997)

WORLD CUP RECORDS

Debutants in the World Cup, France '98 will be a huge adventure for Jamaica – a country which, when the qualifying process started, could never have dreamed of making it to the finals. They had to play ten pre-qualifying matches to reach the CONCACAF final group where one goal scored, two draws and two defeats – including a 6-0 thrashing by Mexico – did not augur well. But from then on in, Jamaica were unbeaten and they clinched their place with a creditable draw in the return with Mexico in their last qualifying match.

KEY PLAYERS

DEON BURTON

Age: 21 **Club:** Derby County (England)

◆ He made 62 appearances in four seasons for Portsmouth and cost Derby £1 million.
◆ Born in Reading, Berkshire, he qualifies for Jamaica because his father came from the island.
◆ He scored in his first four World Cup matches against Costa Rica, Canada, USA and El Salvador.

FITZROY SIMPSON **Age:** 28 **Club:** Portsmouth (England)
◆ Born in the English West Country market town of Trowbridge, he has a Jamaican father.
◆ He began as a left winger, but has operated efficiently at right-back for Portsmouth since the 1996–97 season.
◆ He started his career with local League club Swindon before moving to Manchester City for £500,000 in March 1992.

PAUL HALL **Age:** 25 **Club:** Portsmouth (England)
◆ Born in Manchester of a Jamaican father, he started his career with Torquay United.
◆ He paid his own air fare to attend trials for the Jamaican World Cup campaign.
◆ He partnered Deon Burton in a twin attack for Portsmouth but later moved back to operate just behind the front two.

MANAGER *RENE SIMOES*

PROFILE

Attack is the only way, and you would expect little else from a country coached by a Brazilian, Rene Simoes. He has turned the laid-back Reggae Boyz, as Jamaica are known, into a side full of exciting and unexpected football. Simoes has been in charge since 1994 and qualifying for France is a major achievement. No one would expect them to win, but Jamaica will enjoy the experience.

The Grounds

MARSEILLE

England kick off their campaign in the deep south of France against Tunisia in Marseille, the largest port on the Mediterranean. A city that is a cosmopolitan mix, both in appearance and inhabitants, Marseille is the cultural centre of southern France and boasts more theatres per capita than anywhere else in the country. In terms of appearance, industrial docks stand beside a city centre that is both ancient and picturesque, dating back 2,600 years. There should be no trouble finding your way around because signposts in six different languages have been installed.

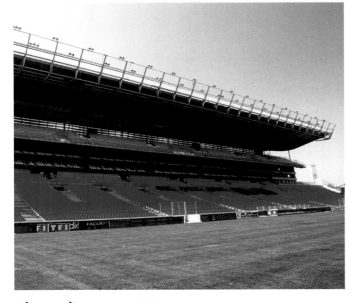

The stadium: Stade Vélodrome.
The refurbished Vélodrome now has a 60,000 all-seated capacity and it is found right in the heart of the city. Home to Olympique Marseille, the locals are devoted football fans.
Getting there: Regular flights from England, five hours by train from Paris.
The matches: France v South Africa (12 June), *England* v Tunisia (15 June), Holland v South Korea (20 June), Brazil v Norway (23 June).

TOULOUSE

Just 60 miles from the Spanish border, with the Spanish influence strongly felt in the bars and restaurants, this is the fourth biggest city in France and a university town. Toulouse University was founded in 1229 and a quarter of the inhabitants are students. Its most striking feature is the pink brick buildings in the Capitole and Daurade areas. Toulouse is a strong rugby area.

The stadium: Stadium Municipal.
Oval-shaped and situated on an island between two branches of the River Garonne, the ground is still centrally located and has been refurbished. There were 34,000 places, many with a restricted view. Now there are 37,000 sheltered seats, all with a clear view. Ground shared by rugby and football teams.
Getting there: Regular flights from England, five trains a day from Paris – five hour journey.
The matches: Cameroon v Austria (11 June), Argentina v Japan (14 June), South Africa v Denmark (18 June), Romania v *England* (22 June), Nigeria v Paraguay (24 June).

LENS

The closest location to England, Lens, in the Nord Pas de Calais region, was a major battleground area on the Western Front in the Great War. Today, cemeteries remind visitors of the past. Until the 1960s it was a huge coal-mining area but recession saw the mines close and now new technology has made its mark. Lens is the smallest of the cities hosting World Cup matches, but has an enthusiastic following and a young audience – 41 per cent of the locals are under 25.

The stadium: Stade Félix Bollaert. Renovated to become an all-seat stadium. The capacity has dropped from almost 52,000 to 41,275, but the tight ground – found 15 minutes away from the centre of Lens – is a favourite with French footballers because of its friendly atmosphere.

Getting there: Fly to Paris and then by train, one hour journey. Otherwise take Eurostar direct to Lille, the neighbouring city.

The matches: Saudi Arabia v Denmark (12 June), Jamaica v Croatia (14 June), Germany v Yugoslavia (21 June), Spain v Bulgaria (24 June), Colombia v *England* (26 June).

PARIS ST DENIS

Home for the World Cup Final, the purpose-built stadium cost £100 million and seats 80,000. Founded in a suburb of Paris, the high-tech facility has 50 bars on-site. An industrial location where Siemens and Panasonic have bases, the World Cup has led to a considerable regeneration of the area. Named after Denis, the first bishop of Lutetia who, according to legend, was beheaded at Monmartre in the third century and walked to St Denis with his head under his arm.

The stadium: Stade de France.
A state of the art construction, the facilities are geared towards the comforts of spectators and players and it is a multi-purpose arena with a maximum audience capacity of 105,000. Surrounded by a running track, the design of the stands is such that the configuration can be made to suit the needs of the event being held.

Getting there: Regular flights to Paris, St Denis is on the airport side of the city. Also Eurostar.

The matches: Brazil v Scotland (10 June), Holland v Belguim (13 June), France v Saudi Arabia (18 June), Italy v Austria (23 June), Romania v Tunisia (26 June).

BORDEAUX

Anyone who strolls round a supermarket will know Bordeaux is wine country – some 500 million bottles are produced here. In the region are the famous vineyards of Graves and Sauternes, Medoc, Pomerol and St Emillon. Described by Victor Hugo as 'Versailles with a pinch of Antwerp', Bordeaux was an outpost of the Roman Empire, although prosperity really arrived in the 18th century. The Garonne river flows through the sedate town which comes dramatically alive when the local football team is doing well.

The stadium: Parc de Lescure.
A national heritage monument, the Parc de Lescure was opened for a World Cup quarter-final match in 1938. There are 32,500 seats, of which only 15,000 are under cover, but the weather is normally good. Centrally located, it is just over a mile from the station and town centre.

Getting there: There is a local airport which takes direct flights from Gatwick, otherwise hourly trains run from Paris – the journey takes three hours.
The matches: Italy v Chile (11 June), Scotland v Norway (16 June), Belgium v Mexico (20 June), South Africa v Saudi Arabia (24 June), Argentina v Croatia (26 June).

LYON

The second-largest city in France, Lyon is a blend of the old (quaint cobbled streets) and the modern (the most impressive art gallery outside Paris). Famous for silk weaving, Lyon is the oldest archeological site outside Rome and was built on a hill by the Rhone river. It was here that the Lumière brothers first brought the cinema to life. Over four million tourists visit the area every year and the football ground hosted two matches in the 1997 Tournoi de France.

The stadium: Stade de Gerland.
Another ground listed as a historical monument. It was designed by Tony Garnier and draws on Roman architecture for its inspiration. There are four symbolic gateways to the grass-banked ground which, in a face-lift, has raised its capacity from 42,000 to 44,000 for the World Cup.
Getting there: Direct flights from the main airports in England. Trains hourly from Paris – journey time, two hours.
The matches: South Korea v Mexico (13 June), Romania v Colombia (15 June), USA v Iran (21 June), France v Denmark (24 June), Japan v Jamaica (26 June).

MONTPELLIER

The world's first medical school was founded in Montpellier, a city which has strong Spanish links and over the years has been at the heart of a religious struggle between Spanish Catholics and Protestants. A halt on the pilgrim road to Santiago de Compostela, Montpellier is famed as a university city which has been attended at varying times by Nostradamus and Rabelais. Now much of the heart of the city is a traffic-free area and Montpellier has a growing place in the French economy. In two decades it has grown from the 21st largest city in the country to the eighth.

The stadium: La Mosson.
Only ten years old, considerable work has been done to improve the stadium which had a small capacity of 30,000, some of which was standing. It can now house 35,000, and there is a homely feel to the ground which can be found in a suburb out of the heart of the city. The improvements to the stadium have reflected the success of the home team.
Getting there: Direct flights or by train – there are five a day from Paris. The journey takes four and a half hours.
The matches: Morocco v Norway (10 June), Paraguay v Bulgaria (12 June), Italy v Cameroon (17 June), Colombia v Tunisia (22 June), Germany v Iran (25 June).

NANTES

A major port on the Atlantic Ocean, the landmark of Nantes is the castle that was once home to the Dukes of Nomandy. Today the city turns out 1,000 engineers every year and is a thriving research centre. Jules Verne was born in Nantes and the surreal art movement first started here. A famous cultural centre, Nantes has an

opera house and runs two festivals, a carnival in the spring and a music festival in June. It is the capital of the Loire region. The football club, Nantes-Atlantique, have won the French championship seven times.

The stadium: Stade de la Beaujoire.
Built in 1984 to host some of the European Championship matches of that year, the 52,000 capacity – of which 17,000 was standing – has been dramatically reduced to make for a 40,000 all-seat stadium. It is located about two miles out of the main city.
Getting there: No direct flights – but it can be reached by air travellers changing in Paris. Otherwise the train – a two-hour journey from the capital.
The matches: Spain v Nigeria (13 June), Brazil v Morocco (16 June), Japan v Croatia (20 June), Chile v Cameroon (23 June), USA v Yugoslavia (25 June)

ST ÉTIENNE

A coal-mining centre in the 19th century, St Étienne has had to reinvent itself to embrace new industries. It was also the centre of France's arms industry and a major manufacturing centre for bicycles. It is more famous, however, for its protected parkland outside the town. The town annually hosts an important book fair.

The stadium: Stade Geoffroy Guichard. Renovated and down-sized to make it an all-seat stadium, the Geoffroy Guichard holds 36,000 spectators. Parking facilities have been increased and there is a new tree-lined access road to the ground.

Getting there: Flights from Britain to Lyon and then a 35-minute journey to St Étienne.

The matches: Yugoslavia v Iran (14 June), Chile v Austria (17 June), Spain v Paraguay (19 June), Scotland v Morocco (23 June), Holland v Mexico (25 June).

PARIS

The City of Light and one of the great capitals of the world, Paris has everything from the finest culture, the Louvre and the Mona Lisa, through to architectural wonders of the world: Notre Dame, the Eiffel Tower, Sacre Coeur. A vibrant night life to cater for all tastes

with high-class opera, classical music, jazz, pop and the cabaret of the Moulin Rouge. Paris is also famous for its restaurants and shopping. Wide boulevards and an efficient underground train system make travelling around easy and Paris is a city always moving with the times.

The stadium: Parc des Princes. Opened in 1972, Parc des Princes now takes second-place to the new St Denis stadium, but is still a vibrant arena for sport. The acoustics of the stadium make for a wall of sound that is so loud it will seem there are more than 49,000 people housed within the concrete structure.

Getting there: Regular flights from Britain and Eurostar to the centre of the city – just two hours from the English Channel.

The matches: Germany v USA (15 June), Nigeria v Bulgaria (19 June), Argentina v Jamaica (21 June), Belgium v South Korea (25 June).

Local kick-off times shown.

Group Stage

	Team	Venue	Time	Winner	Score
A	BRAZIL v SCOTLAND	PARIS SF	10 JUNE 5.30	......	......
	MOROCCO v NORWAY	MONTPELLIER	10 JUNE 9.00	......	......
	NORWAY v SCOTLAND	BORDEAUX	16 JUNE 5.30	......	......
	BRAZIL v MOROCCO	NANTES	16 JUNE 9.00	......	......
	BRAZIL v NORWAY	MARSEILLE	23 JUNE 9.00	......	......
	MOROCCO v SCOTLAND	ST ÉTIENNE	23 JUNE 9.00	......	......
B	CHILE v ITALY	BORDEAUX	11 JUNE 5.30	......	......
	AUSTRIA v CAMEROON	TOULOUSE	11 JUNE 9.00	......	......
	AUSTRIA v CHILE	ST ÉTIENNE	17 JUNE 5.30	......	......
	CAMEROON v ITALY	MONTPELLIER	17 JUNE 9.00	......	......
	AUSTRIA v ITALY	PARIS SF	23 JUNE 4.00	......	......
	CAMEROON v CHILE	NANTES	23 JUNE 4.00	......	......
C	DENMARK v SAUDI ARABIA	LENS	12 JUNE 5.30	......	......
	FRANCE v S. AFRICA	MARSEILLE	12 JUNE 9.00	......	......
	DENMARK v S. AFRICA	TOULOUSE	18 JUNE 5.30	......	......
	FRANCE v SAUDI ARABIA	PARIS SF	18 JUNE 9.00	......	......
	DENMARK v FRANCE	LYON	24 JUNE 4.00	......	......
	SAUDI ARABIA v S. AFRICA	BORDEAUX	24 JUNE 4.00	......	......
D	BULGARIA v PARAGUAY	MONTPELLIER	12 JUNE 2.30	......	......
	NIGERIA v SPAIN	NANTES	13 JUNE 2.30	......	......
	BULGARIA v NIGERIA	PARIS PP	19 JUNE 5.30	......	......
	PARAGUAY v SPAIN	ST ÉTIENNE	19 JUNE 9.00	......	......
	BULGARIA v SPAIN	LENS	24 JUNE 9.00	......	......
	NIGERIA v PARAGUAY	TOULOUSE	24 JUNE 9.00	......	......
E	MEXICO v SOUTH KOREA	LYON	13 JUNE 5.30	......	......
	BELGIUM v HOLLAND	PARIS SF	13 JUNE 9.00	......	......
	BELGIUM v MEXICO	BORDEAUX	20 JUNE 5.30	......	......
	HOLLAND v SOUTH KOREA	MARSEILLE	20 JUNE 9.00	......	......
	HOLLAND v MEXICO	ST ÉTIENNE	25 JUNE 4.00	......	......
	BELGIUM v SOUTH KOREA	PARIS PP	25 JUNE 4.00	......	......
F	IRAN v YUGOSLAVIA	ST ÉTIENNE	14 JUNE 5.30	......	......
	GERMANY v USA	PARIS PP	15 JUNE 9.00	......	......
	GERMANY v YUGOSLAVIA	LENS	21 JUNE 2.30	......	......
	IRAN v USA	LYON	21 JUNE 9.00	......	......
	GERMANY v IRAN	MONTPELLIER	25 JUNE 9.00	......	......
	USA v YUGOSLAVIA	NANTES	25 JUNE 9.00	......	......
G	ENGLAND v TUNISIA	MARSEILLE	15 JUNE 2.30	......	......
	COLOMBIA v ROMANIA	LYON	15 JUNE 5.30	......	......
	GERMANY v TUNISIA	MONTPELLIER	22 JUNE 5.30	......	......
	ENGLAND v ROMANIA	TOULOUSE	22 JUNE 9.00	......	......
	ROMANIA v TUNISIA	PARIS SF	26 JUNE 9.00	......	......
	COLOMBIA v ENGLAND	LENS	26 JUNE 9.00	......	......
H	ARGENTINA v JAPAN	TOULOUSE	14 JUNE 2.30	......	......
	CROATIA v JAMAICA	LENS	14 JUNE 9.00	......	......
	ARGENTINA v JAMAICA	NANTES	20 JUNE 2.30	......	......
	ENGLAND v JAPAN	PARIS PP	21 JUNE 5.30	......	......
	ARGENTINA v CROATIA	BORDEAUX	26 JUNE 4.00	......	......
	JAMAICA v JAPAN	LYON	26 JUNE 4.00	......	......

TOURNAMENT PLANNER FRANCE '98

SECOND ROUND

1 — PARIS PP 27 JUNE 9.00
WINNER OF A / RUNNER-UP OF B — WINNER / SCORE

2 — MARSEILLE 27 JUNE 4.30
WINNER OF B / RUNNER-UP OF A — WINNER / SCORE

3 — LENS 28 JUNE 4.30
WINNER OF C / RUNNER-UP OF D — WINNER / SCORE

4 — PARIS SF 28 JUNE 9.00
WINNER OF D / RUNNER-UP OF C — WINNER / SCORE

5 — TOULOUSE 29 JUNE 9.00
WINNER OF E / RUNNER-UP OF F — WINNER / SCORE

6 — MONTPELLIER 29 JUNE 4.30
WINNER OF F / RUNNER-UP OF E — WINNER / SCORE

7 — BORDEAUX 30 JUNE 4.30
WINNER OF G / RUNNER-UP OF H — WINNER / SCORE

8 — ST ÉTIENNE 30 JUNE 9.00
WINNER OF H / RUNNER-UP OF G — WINNER / SCORE

QUARTER-FINALS

A — NANTES 3 JULY 9.00
WINNER OF 1 / WINNER OF 4 — WINNER / SCORE

B — PARIS SF 3 JULY 4.30
WINNER OF 2 / WINNER OF 3 — WINNER / SCORE

C — MARSEILLE 4 JULY 4.30
WINNER OF 5 / WINNER OF 8 — WINNER / SCORE

D — LYON 4 JULY 9.00
WINNER OF 6 / WINNER OF 7 — WINNER / SCORE

SEMI-FINALS

MARSEILLE 7 JULY 9.00
WINNER OF A / WINNER OF C — WINNER / SCORE

PARIS SF 8 JULY 9.00
WINNER OF B / WINNER OF D — WINNER / SCORE

THIRD PLACE FINAL

PARIS PP 11 JULY 9.00
WINNER / SCORE

WORLD CUP FINAL

PARIS SF 12 JULY 9.00

WORLD CHAMPIONS